TABLE OF CONTENTS

The Mind of A Con Man
The Psychology of Lying
©Copyright 2013 by Dr. Leland Benton

DISCLAIMER AND TERMS OF USE AGREEMENT:

(Please Read This Before Using This Book)

This information is for educational and informational purposes only. The content is not intended to be a substitute for any professional advice, diagnosis, or treatment.

The author and publisher of this book and the accompanying materials have used their best efforts in preparing this book.

The author and publisher make no representation or warranties with respect to the accuracy, applicability, fitness, or completeness of the contents of this book. The information contained in this book is strictly for educational purposes. Therefore, if you wish to apply

Who is fooling who? This isn't a book you have ever read before but it is a book you should read! I am going to take you on an adventure into the human mind and show you not only why con men do what they do but why you do the things you do too.

I'm Dr. Leland Benton and I have two outstanding qualifications to write this book. I have been a doctor of behavioral science and Chief Forensic Investigator for ForensicsNation for over 32-years. I have hunted down and caused the arrest of hundreds of con men and my behavioral science training has assisted me in profiling their behavior, habits, and modus operandi.

I will not only describe Type 1 Con Men who are professional con men that purposely prey on individuals for some type of gain – money, power, sex, etc but I will also describe Type 2 Con Men that you come into contact daily.

These people are manipulators and can be anyone from your mommy, family members, and friends to co-workers, sales people and advertisers in general. Type 2 individuals are quite different from Type 1 individuals.

Type 1 individuals are professionals at practicing their deceptive trade for pecuniary gain. Fortunately you may never come into contact with a Bernie Madoff or Frank Abagnale but you do come into contact with Type 2 individuals daily.

These people are what I call amateur con men, who attempt to manipulate you into doing something they want you to do. Candidly, Type 2 individuals are more dangerous than Type 1 individuals.

The "con game" (the word "con" is short for "confidence") is a worldwide pandemic problem. No country or race of people is immune to the con game. Dictators are nothing more than con men deceiving whole countries into believing something they want them to believe.

Islamic fanaticism and Arab fundamentalism is the most preemptive con game going today. Using religion, Arab leaders have conned Muslims worldwide into believing a false doctrine and the blood flows red from their evil deception.

Closer to home, the con game seemingly appears nightly on the evening news and makes good copy too. Here is a recent article of what is fast becoming an epidemic of the con game within academia:

http://www.nytimes.com/2013/04/28/magazine/diederik-stapels-audacious-academic-fraud.html?nl=todaysheadlines&emc=edit_th_20130428

The article is rather long but it is a real eye-opener and one that only briefly touches on the con game within academia. You can bet there is more to uncover.

I will first give you a brief lesson in behavioral science in Chapter 1 in order to allow you to better understand yourself as well as the mind of a con man in general.

I will then move swiftly into describing Type 1 and Type 2 individuals that use the con game tactics.

The remaining chapters deal with the psychology of lying, living in a fantasy world and how to spot a con man and manipulator.

This book is part of my Cyber Crime/Cyber Forensics book series, which I have written to protect individuals from various crimes.

Confessions of a Child Predator
http://www.amazon.com/dp/B007BB97KU
Child Watch
http://www.amazon.com/dp/B0095K1P3M

Cyber-Daters Beware
http://www.amazon.com/dp/B006J9T4NA
Cyber Protect Your Business
http://www.amazon.com/dp/B0095JEAYY
ForensicsNation Bushwhacker Program
http://www.amazon.com/dp/B007I9AHVS
ForensicsNationsStore.com Catalog
http://ForensicsNationStore.com
Protecting Yourself from Cyber Crime
http://www.amazon.com/dp/B0095J3EIW
Stealing You
http://www.amazon.com/dp/B00778TT6E
Was Sandy Hook a Hoax?
http://www.amazon.com/dp/B00BFSM8IS
Why Women Should Not Use Online Dating Services
http://www.amazon.com/dp/B006J9EMH8
You Can Run But You Cannot Hide
http://www.amazon.com/dp/B006JLVZC6

It is also a book that is part of my "Why" series of books
that address individual human behavioral traits and I
strongly recommend these books to get a more in depth
study of a specific trait.

Why You Do The Things You Do Book 1
http://www.amazon.com/dp/B00BG9FLNA
Why You Are Greedy Book 2
http://www.amazon.com/dp/B00BGLZT8K
Why You Are Immoral Book 3
http://www.amazon.com/dp/B00BH1O7GO
Why You Are In Debt Up To Your Eyeballs Book 4
http://www.amazon.com/dp/B00BHUBHMW
Why You Are Lonely Book 5

So, who is fooling who? Better yet, who is fooling YOU? We shall see so sit back for the adventure. You are never going to be the same again…

Chapter 1 – Laying A Proper Foundation

In all of my "Why" series of books, I will provide the following discourse on the Human Mind in order to lay a proper foundation to what I am about to teach.

The Mechanism of the Human Mind

Which Comes First - the Body or the Mind?

(the most important concept in all of talk therapy)

© 2007, Steven Paglierani, The Center for Emergence

Understanding the Body - Mind Connection

For thousands of years, we have known there is a body – mind connection. Until now though, we have not known what this connection is. What it it? Time. The body and the mind each have their own sense of time. Their own clocks so to speak. Therapy works only when these two clocks are in sync.

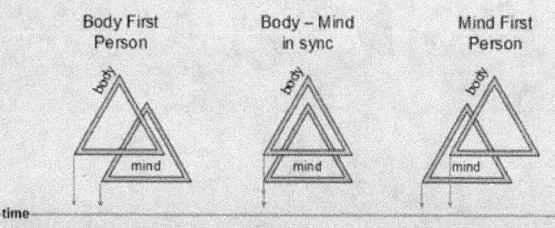

Body First
Person

Body – Mind
in sync

Mind First
Person

time

Prior to the fall of man into sin as described in the Garden of Eden, man's spirit was hooked to God's infinite spirit. There was no death because God's spirit is infinite. Man is the only animal on earth that shares the eternality nature of God. The subject of eternal life has been a heated topic of man from the beginning of our existence.

In Greek mythology, there's a story about a mortal youth named Tithonus. Aurora, the goddess of dawn, fell in love with the boy and when Zeus, the king of the gods, promised to grant Aurora any gift she chose for her lover, she asked that Tithonus might live forever. But, in her haste she forgot to ask for eternal youth, so when Zeus granted her request, Tithonus was doomed to an eternity of perpetual aging as a grouchy old man… forever.

In the movie "Highlander," Angus McLeod was born in 1518 as an immortal being. He could not die and to me, the best part of the movie was the depiction of this immortal's agony here on earth as he watched everything he loved die forcing him to begin his life over and over again. He saw all of the ugliness, which man had caused over four centuries. He witnessed the Spanish Inquisition, Waterloo, the atrocities of the Third Reich, and more. He saw the slavery and bigotry of the eighteenth century, the slaughter of the Native American tribes after the Civil War. This man's life was a living Hell!

There is a very big difference between the ways our feeble minds picture eternal life versus God's idea of eternal life. Our understanding comes from Quantum Physics and is limited within the Time-Space Continuum.

11

Life is your spirit, but the soul of man has usurped the spirit's position and psychology is now forced to define "how" we live our lives based on the animating force of the soul instead of the spirit. As I said previously, the soul has usurped the spirit's place as our animating force. Let's discuss this now.

- ❖ **Body First Person** - When the body becomes our life, we live as animals.
- ❖ **Body-Mind In Sync -** When the soul becomes our life, we live as rebels and fugitives in a life of desires, emotions, and will (consuming entities). This is the position of mankind today!
- ❖ **Mind First Person** - But when we come to live our life in the mind/spirit and by the spirit, though we still use our soul's faculties just as we do our physical faculties, they are now the servants of the spirit.

If you live as a consuming entity, you will always lose. In other words, to get, you must give - you must sacrifice! Have you ever wondered why you have so many anxieties, phobias, worries and fears? The reality of this world is evil. So what is reality? I will tell you. This is reality:

"Life without war is impossible either in nature or in grace. The basis of physical, mental, moral and spiritual life is antagonism. Health is the balance between physical life and external nature, and it is maintained only by sufficient vitality on the inside against things on the outside. Everything outside my physical life is designed to put me to death. Things, which keep me going when I

12

am alive, disintegrate me when I am dead. If I have enough fighting power, I produce the balance of health.

The same is true of mental life. If I want to maintain a vigorous mental life, I have to fight, and in that way the mental balance called thought is produced. Morally it is the same. Everything that does not partake of the nature of virtue is the enemy of virtue in me, and it depends on what moral caliber I have whether I overcome and produce virtue (GOOD CHARACTER). Immediately I fight, I am moral in that particular. No man is virtuous because he cannot help it; virtue (character) is acquired.

❖ Psychology only studies the observable aspects of the mind and discounts the unseen or intangible aspects of the human mind.
❖ Behavioral science attempts to study the intangible aspects of the human mind…why you do the things you do and more importantly why you don't do what you should do.
❖ There is no such thing as commercial psychology versus personal psychology. The mind uses the same mechanism to evaluate all types of relationships.
❖ Everything we do revolves around relationships. We relate to our environment, our friends, family, co-workers, other people and even our pets. We are social animals.

The Mechanism of the Human Mind

Belief Systems + Thought + Delight = Action/Behavior/Conduct

Conscious Mind

5-senses:
Sight
Hearing
Taste
Touch
Smell
ESP (women only)

Subconscious Mind

Intellect:
Experiential
Empirical

DEW:
Desires, Emotions and Will

The Human Psyche Differences Between Genders

The female psyche operates on emotional, spiritual, physical and intellectual planes
The male psyche operates only on the intellectual and physical planes.

Here is an exercise you might find weird but it demonstrates the power of the human mind.

Fi yuo cna raed tihs, yuo hvae a sgtrane mnid too. Cna yuo raed tihs? Olny 55 plepoe out of 100 can. I cdnuolt blveiee taht I cluod aulaclty uesdnatnrd waht I was rdanieg. The phaonmneal pweor of the hmuan

mnid, aoccdrnig to a rscheearch at Cmabrigde Uinervtisy, it dseno't mtaetr in waht oerdr the ltteres in a wrod are, the olny iproamtnt tihng is taht the frsit and lsat ltteer be in the rghit pclae. The rset can be a taotl mses and you can sitll raed it whotuit a pboerlm. Tihs is bcuseae the huamn mnid deos not raed ervey lteter by istlef, but the wrod as a wlohe. Azanmig huh? Yaeh and I awlyas tghuhot slpeling was ipmorantt!

You might have found it somewhat unusual that you could probably read the jumbled mess above. Actually over half the people that see this exercise can decipher the words at the same speed of reading as if the words were not jumbled.

It is important to note that the human mind thinks in packages...concepts rather than individual ideas.

Your eyes see each letter but the mind looks at the whole word instead. As you read, the mind looks at the first and last letter only. Remember this; the mind sees the beginning and end. We will talk about this later...

If you were to listen to an orchestra, your ear listens to every note from every instrument but a trained ear can actually pick out individual instruments from the whole sound as the mind hears the whole symphony.

How does this apply to you?

Learning to observe means going beyond the mind's natural ability to only read the first and last letters of a word!

It is training the mind to see all the letters, not just the eye but the mind!

Truisms About the Human Mind

- ❖ Pain vs. Pleasure – people are more motivated to avoid pain than seek pleasure.
- ❖ A person that is suffering depression will seek relief (notice I didn't say cure) before they seek happiness.
- ❖ The human mind cannot tell the difference between fantasy and reality.
- ❖ The human mind gravitates to the desires, emotions and will of its psyche. People crave entertainment so fantasy dominates their existences.
- ❖ The human mind is easily distracted! You can either be the cause of these distractions or other stimuli will be the cause but rest assured people WILL BE distracted because the human mind is gullible.

The human mind responds quickly to these three forms of stimuli

- ❖ Sex
- ❖ Humor
- ❖ FEAR

But the greatest of them all is FEAR!

BTW – on the positive side we have faith, hope, love, but the greatest of these *is* LOVE.

Fear usually takes the form of what is called "Scarcity Thought"

You are afraid that someone will have what you feel belongs to you or that others will have more "stuff" than you.

❖ The subconscious mind is often referred to as the "heart," and is the control mechanism the body uses to store our beliefs.

❖ **These beliefs are stored as pictures in our "hearts" and create frequencies in our bodies.**

❖ We know that the optimum human frequency is a little below 7.83 hertz. To drop below this frequency brings on the onslaught of disease. To rise above it a person demonstrates psychic abilities.

❖ Harmful beliefs that cause unhealthy frequencies are the source of almost all problems - physical, mental, emotional.

❖ The subconscious mind creates a belief system, which we call "pictures of the heart."

❖ These pictures involve either visions, or dreams/fantasies.

❖ Science has discovered that the subconscious mind cannot distinguish between fantasy and reality.

*The subject of all dreams is the dreamer.
*Dreams are born in our desires, emotions and will.
*Dreamers believe in a belief system, which is fantasy.
*A life lived within a fantasy creates a feeling of self-centeredness, hopelessness and despair. In dreams everything is perfect.
*The subject of a vision is not the visionary but the world.
*Visions are born in the intellect.
*Visions are pictures of the future that have already been experienced in the heart of those who give it birth.
*Visionaries sacrifice themselves for the good of mankind.
*Visions have a moral quality that transcends the self-centered nature of dreams.
*By its very nature a vision launches a mission, a "cause-that-inspires."
*Visions create a sense of belonging.

❖ We act upon visions and/or dreams, using thought.
❖ Thought employs the intellect, in the case of visions, or the desires, emotions and the will, in the case of dreams.
❖ Intellectual thought relies on wisdom; emotional thought relies on the pursuit of pleasure, comfort and delight.
❖ Dreamers live within a facade; they create a false sense of worth using imaginary situations.

- ❖ Visionaries live within reality; they create change, within a framework of restraint, and intellectual thought.
- ❖ The world is made up of OPPOSITES, which is usually the corrupted version of the original. We have good and evil. We have love and lust!
- ❖ EVERYTHING YOU DO IS BECAUSE OF LOVE OR LUST. Learn to love because there are no crimes beyond forgiveness.

*Love is born in the intellect; lust is born in the DEW!
*Love is vision; lust is fantasy.
*Love restrains & sacrifices; lust is selfish
*Love is being one with someone or something
*Lust is being with someone or something.
*Visionaries love; dreamers lust!
*Visionaries do what is required; dreamers just do their best!

WHEN THERE IS NO HOPE OF LOVE DO WE ABANDON OURSELVES TO LUST?

Yes we do!

Pictures of the heart are your belief system.

- ❖ We animate these pictures into either fantasies, or visions.
- ❖ People do not appear to see the difference between the matter part of an organism and the life part, which animates it.

❖ We seem to think that the organism itself is life. In other words, it is not our outward appearance that is our life, but our inward existence.

❖ Life is what goes into the body. Death is what comes out.

❖ A person who lies is not a liar because he tells a lie. The lie is the manifested behavior of some subconscious belief system. The lie only demonstrates that the person is a liar…it is the effect.

❖ Except for love, the power of words inspired by a vision or fantasy is the most potent human force.

"Do you want to have or do you want to be?"

*For a dreamer: "Seeing is believing!"
*But they only see imaginary things that are not real!!
*This is why "The Secret" is WRONG!
*Say it and claim it is WRONG!
*Blab it and grab it IS WRONG!
*See it and be it IS WRONG!
Dreamers practice companionship – To be with someone or something!

VERY IMPORTANT:

1. Dreamers covet the object of their temptation, BUT they covet <u>the temptation</u> more so than <u>the object</u> itself because <u>the temptation is the idol of their fantasy</u>.

2. If there is a conflict between the conscious and subconscious mind, the subconscious mind always wins…ALWAYS!

3. All reaction occurs in the conscious mind; all interaction occurs in the subconscious mind. Fear is a "REACTION" to losing control.

For a visionary: "Believing is seeing!"

There are no SECRETS; there are only challenges to be conquered!

THIS IS NOT A SECRET: Putting a photo of a Ferrari on your refrigerator and seeing yourself driving it by employing the so-called law of attraction is pure BUPKES!!! Why? Because this is all occurring in the conscious mind and beliefs reside in the subconscious mind. How do you transfer something from the conscious mind to the subconscious mind and make it a belief system?

A Ferrari is the object of your temptation but what you covet most is the temptation of owning a Ferrari because the temptation is the idol of your fantasy.

It is all about ATTENTION & ACCEPTANCE!!!!! I have a $100 bill in my hand and I am willing to give it to you. But if you don't ACCEPT it then it is still in my hand. BELIEF SYSTEMS ARE CREATED BY ATTENTION & ACCEPTANCE!

John 1:12 But as many as received him, to them gave he **the right** to become children of God, *even* to them that believe on his name

Human things must be known to be loved; but divine things must be loved to be known.

BELIEVING IS SEEING!

Let's talk about goals...which of the following goals are good goals?

❖ To want to get married and have a wonderful, happy, loving marriage?
❖ To want to have children who are happy, successful, and loving?
❖ To have a successful, fulfilling and rewarding career?
❖ Is it a good goal to want to have fun, bonded, loving, and meaningful relationships with other people?

Which of the listed goals are good goals? None of them!

You should never have anything for a goal that is not 100% under your control, AND each and every goal should be motivated by love.

Almost all goals that we have in our life are wrong.

Everything that we do, we do because of a goal we have.

When we get up in the morning, it's because of some goal that we have; we are hungry for breakfast, or we need to go to work.

If we go to the grocery store, it's because of some goal we have. If we are kind to people, it's because of some goal that we have.

Now we don't always know what they are, because a lot of these are subconscious goals.

The goals we have are the reasons for everything we do. But, do all of your goals involve only YOU?

Of course not!

And when the other person, or persons, in your goal do not perform, or act the way you want them to, then we become anxious and stressed.

When our goals get blocked, it creates anger, anxiety, and frustration. If we only have good goals, we will not experience anger or anxiety.

That's how you know, if you are living a wrongful goal. If the result is anger and frustration because your control was blocked and blocking your goal, then you had a wrongful goal. It may have been a fine and noble desire, but a wrongful goal.

Filters

We live in a society of consumerism and entertainment. In my previous books I have spoken reams about this subject. Instant gratification is paramount and today's technology delivers information and other stimuli in bucketfuls to the human mind. We have already spoken about filters that the human mind employs to weed out what it determines to be irrelevant. This "irrelevancy" is different in every individual and many times is programmed into our minds subconsciously or without us knowing it. We have also spoken about the causes of these various filters such as environment, maturity, upbringing, culture, etc.

The one essential common element of all filters is that they are all ATTENTION diverters. We have spoken about attention earlier; what is very interesting is that filters are generally viewed as bad when some are really very good.

I had a friend, who lives in Chicago, fall on hard times and needed assistance. When I got to him he was living in a cheap hotel and had a room so small when you put the key in the door you broke the *window (I slay me)*. His room was about 50 feet from the Loop (the overhead train that circles around Chicago). The noise was deafening when the train went by, and it went by often, but my friend had filtered it out. Amazing, but when you thing about it, my friend really does hear the train but yet he pays no attention to it, so in actuality, it is like he doesn't hear it at all! So filters divert attention, and take away our focus; so let's talk about focus.

The Incredible Power of Focus
One of the more important points I have made has been the idea that you really do create your own life and your own reality. I know this idea has become a kind of personal growth cliché that many of us have heard over and over for years. Many people, after continuing to experience the same old ups and downs and personal dramas over many years, get to the point where they dismiss this idea as charming but useless -- or just plain

wrong. "If I'm creating this, then I'm certainly not doing it on purpose," they say. "It sure seems like this is HAPPENING to me, rather than that I'm creating it." They just assume that it's all BS because "this and this and this and this are going on for me, and I have no control over it, and anyone who thinks I'm creating this doesn't understand what I'm going through." Essentially, they are resigning themselves to becoming a victim of circumstances.

We live in a universe of infinite complexity and many forces -- way too many to keep track of -- operate on us. Yes, it is true that we are NOT in control of everything that happens, because we are not in control of most of those infinite other parts of the universe. In fact, the only thing you have total and complete control over is...YOUR OWN MIND. That is, if you learn how to exercise it.

Luckily, this one thing -- your mind -- that you do have control over gives you tremendous power. By exercising control over your mind, you can get the rest of those infinite other parts of the universe to begin to march in formation.

The person who says, "If I'm creating this, it certainly isn't on purpose," is right. They are not creating what is happening to them "on purpose." Who would purposely create failure, or bad relationships, or any other kind of suffering? You can only do something that is not good for you that is harmful to you, if you do it subconsciously. This means if you are creating something you don't want, you must be doing so subconsciously.

Your mind is running on automatic pilot, based on "software" (subconscious programming) installed when you were too young to know any better, by parents,

25

teachers, friends, the media, and other experiences and influences. The key is to become more conscious, more aware...to get yourself off automatic pilot. Once you do this, you stop creating all the dramas and other garbage you don't want in your life.

How do you do this? One way is by remembering and using a very important piece of wisdom. What is this important piece of wisdom? I'm glad you asked.

It's the fact that whatever you focus on manifests as reality in your life.

You are always focusing on something, whether you are aware of it or not. If I spent some time with you, and heard your history, I could tell you what you are focusing on. How? By looking at the results you are getting in your life. The results you get are always the result of your focus.

The problem is this focus is usually not conscious focus; it's automatic or subconscious focus. We subconsciously focus on something we don't want, and then when we get it we feel like a victim and don't even stop to think that we created it in the first place. And what is more, we don't realize we could choose to create something completely different if we could only get out of the cycle of subconsciously focusing on something other than what we want.

If you have a significant negative emotional experience (say, for instance, a relationship in which you are abused or mistreated in some way), a part of you is going to say: "Okay, I get it. There are people out there who can and will hurt me. Relationships can be dangerous and painful. I have to watch out for these people [or sometimes,

26

relationships in general] and avoid them." Unfortunately, to watch out for them and avoid them, you have to focus your mind on "people who could hurt me," or "bad relationships," and that focus draws more of what you don't want to you...AND...actually makes these things you don't want (at least initially) attractive to you, so when they appear in your life you are drawn to them. This is why many people keep having one relationship after another with the same person, but in different bodies. This, of course, applies to everything, not just relationships. I'm just using relationships as an example.

Focusing on what you do not want, ironically, makes it happen. Focusing on not being poor makes you poor. Focusing on not making mistakes causes you to make mistakes. Focusing on not having a bad relationship creates bad relationships. Focusing on not being depressed makes you depressed. Focusing on not smoking makes you want to smoke. And so on. I think you get the idea. The mind will create what you focus on both GOOD and BAD!!!

The truth is your mind cannot tell the difference between something you think about or focus on that you DO want, and something you think about or focus on but Do NOT want. The mind is a goal-seeking mechanism, and an extremely effective one at that. Already, all the time, it is elegantly and precisely creating exactly what you focus on. You are already a World Champion Expert at creating whatever you focus on. You couldn't get any better at it, and you don't need to get any better at it.

When you focus on anything, your mind says: "Okay, we can do that," and starts figuring out how to do it. It doesn't ask whether you're focusing on it because you want it or because you do not want it. It ALWAYS assumes you want what you focus on and then it goes and makes it happen. The more frequent and the more intense the focus, the faster and more completely you will create what you have focused on, which is why intense negative experiences create intense focus on what you do not want, and tend to make you re-create what you don't want, over and over.

Most of the time, for most people, all the focusing and thinking is going by at warp speed, on automatic, without much, if any, conscious intention. Your job is to learn how to direct this power by consciously directing your focus to the outcomes you want. Once you do, everything changes. This does, however, take some work, because at first you have to swim upstream against the current of your old, unconscious habits, and the current can be swift and strong. Trained observation actually teaches you to focus on what you want.

First, you have to discover all the things you focus on that you do not want, and I'm willing to bet there are quite a few -- way more than you think. To the degree you're getting what you don't want, you are focusing, albeit subconsciously, on what you don't want.

Spend some time over the next few weeks making a list of all the things you do NOT want as you notice yourself thinking about them.

Second, you have to get very clear about what you DO want. Then, you have to examine each of the things you want and be sure they are not just something you do NOT want in disguise. For instance, saying "I want a relationship where I am treated well" would not even be an issue if you had not had relationships where you were not treated well, and even in making this seemingly positive statement you are focusing on not wanting to be mistreated. Saying "I want a reliable car" wouldn't even come up if you weren't focusing on the fact that you don't want a car that breaks down and needs a lot of repairs.

After you've sorted out the things you habitually focus on that you do not want, and know what you do want, you have to begin to notice each time you think about an outcome you do not want, and consciously change your thinking, right in that moment, so you are instead focusing on what you do want.

Remember, you do NOT have to avoid things to be happy and get what you want. The urge to avoid something is a result of having had a negative emotional experience regarding that thing, and trying to avoid things requires you to focus on them, which tells your brain to create them. Not good.

You will be surprised how often you are thinking about what you do not want, how difficult it is to catch yourself doing it every time, and -- most of all – how difficult it is to switch your thinking to what you DO want. There is a strong momentum to keep thinking about that thing you want to avoid. As I said, the current is strong and swift, especially at first.

The solution? Practice, practice, practice. Persistence, persistence, persistence!!!

It's a very good idea to write down what you want, very specifically, so that your Fairy Godmother, were she to read it, would know exactly what to give you without any additional explanation.

Then, read what you have written to yourself, preferably out loud, several times a day, while seeing yourself, in your mind, already having what you want.

Believing is seeing and not the other way around as the world teaches you!

The more emotion you can bring to it, the better. Then, take whatever action is available to begin moving toward what you want. A good time to do this reading and visualizing is when you first wake up and before you go to bed.

I know this is work. Do it anyway. There is a price for everything, and this is the price you must pay to get what you want. Be prepared to pay it. It will be worth it, I promise. And be prepared to pay for a while before you get results. Stick with it.

Another way to change your focus is to ask questions. As an example, I'll ask you one right now. What did you have for breakfast this morning? To answer this question (even to just internally process the question), you had to shift your focus from whatever your mind was focused on (hopefully, to what I am teaching) to today's breakfast.

This means that to change your focus, all you have to do is...ask yourself a question!

It also means you better be careful what questions you ask yourself. Good questions include "How can I get X?" "How can I do X?" "How can I be X?" By asking these kinds of questions, you get your mind to focus on what you want to have, do, or be. Then, your mind takes over and answers the question...solves the problem...and creates what you want. You just have to provide the focus, take whatever action presents itself, and be persistent (some things take time).

I would do away with questions like "What's wrong with me?" or "Why can't I find someone to love me?" and so on. Your mind will find an answer to any question you give it, including these disempowering questions.

Learn to say "How can I...?" when you don't know what to do, instead of "I can't," and (if you are persistent in asking) you will receive the answer, every time. Learn to be conscious in what you focus on and your whole life will change.

This all may seem very utopian to you, or overly simplistic, or like a lot of work. I assure you it is not utopian (it's the way all successful people think), it IS simple, but not simplistic, and yes, it is work, at first. The great Napoleon Hill, who spent over 60 years studying the most effective and most successful people of the 20th century, concluded that -- without exception -- "whatever the mind can conceive and believe, it can achieve." He at first suspected there had to be exceptions, but toward the end of his life he said he had to admit he had not found ANY.

Let's go over that again: "Whatever the mind can conceive and believe it can achieve."

It will take some time to learn how to consciously focus your mind. It will require some effort. You will fail many times, and it will seem difficult. But at a certain point you will "get it" and at that point it will become as automatic as the unconscious focusing you have been doing. When that happens, a whole new universe of power will open to you.

More on Focusing

"And be not conformed to this age, but be transformed by the renewing of your mind, in order to prove by you what is the good and pleasing and perfect will of God."

The one thing in your life you can command is your own mind. Whatever negative people and situations you face, you can always choose a positive attitude. But doing so requires a firm, strong commitment.

Helpful: Begin by writing a self-convincing creed – I believe I can direct and control my emotions, intellect and habits with the intention of developing a positive mental attitude. Post it where you'll see it when you get up in the morning. Read it during the day, and say it aloud. Speaking an intention reinforces it. Choose a "self-motivator" – a meaningful phrase tailored to help you reach your positive thinking goals. Examples:

- Counter discouragement with the phrase "Every problem contains the seed of its own solution."

- Fight procrastination with "Do it now."

Keep your self-motivators nearby – in your pocket or on your desk – and repeat them throughout the day to instill these important new values.

Develop A Life Plan. Setting short and long-term goals each day creates a road map for your life. But only set GOOD goals!!! What is a good goal? One where you are 100% in control and one that is founded in love! A goal of raising good, healthy and prosperous children is a bad goal because you are not in control of what your kids choose. See the important difference? The goal is noble but it is not a good goal.

You identify where you're going, focus your mind on getting there and avoid many wrong turns.

Helpful: Use the D-E-S-I-R-E formula as a goal-setting guideline...

- **D**etermine what you want. Be exact, and express the goal positively. Say what you want to be or do rather than what you don't want.

- **E**valuate what you'll give in return. How much work will you do to turn your plan into action?

- **S**et a date for your goal. Be realistic, allowing enough time without postponing it too long.

- **I**dentify a step by step plan. Devise immediate, small steps to get started.

- **R**epeat your plan in writing.

- **E**ach and every day, morning and evening, read your plan aloud as you picture yourself already having achieved your goals.

Writing out your daily goals helps maintain your motivation. Keep them in your pocket or purse to read frequently throughout the day.

The Power of Visualization
Because visual images reach into our deepest mental levels, I have found pictures to be profound motivational tools. Why? Remember the mind holds everything as pictures!

Helpful: Make a list of personal qualities you want to develop...write down the names of people with whom you would like to have better relationships. Now clip pictures from magazines and newspapers that symbolize your goals.

Example: If generosity is your chosen quality, you could use a photo of someone with an outstretched hand.

Put the pictures where you'll see them everyday…and believe that you will get what you have visualized. You may also create your own "mental pictures" to defeat negative thoughts, such as dwelling on past reversals. Maintain A Positive Focus. Giving yourself positive experiences actually reinforces your positive attitude. Examples…

- Treat your five senses every day. Listen to your favorite music, taste a food you love, enjoy a beautiful view, etc.

- Cultivate a sense of humor. Laughter relaxes tension, and seeing the funny side of things helps you take yourself less seriously.

- Smile when you feel like frowning. Smile at yourself in the mirror. If this makes you laugh at yourself, the smile will be that much more real.

Now realize the optimistic face you show the world creates positive thoughts about you in everyone you meet.

How to Train Your Subconscious Mind
Did you know that often the difference between success and failure is the ability to train your mind to focus on achieving your goals and not focus on problems? It's been proven by researchers and by some of the most successful people in the world.

Getting your mind to focus and concentrate on success - so that it finds solutions instead of focusing on the problems is usually the difference between success and failure. But how do you do this?

I'm about to show you how. I'll outline the importance of training your mind, how to start directing your subconscious mind, and how to keep your mind focused so that you constantly achieve your goals and live the life you want. Disciplining your mind so that it is focused on your goals is crucial to your success. If your mind is not trained to focus on and achieve your goals then you really have little chance of success. Your conscious mind is a direct link to your subconscious mind.

So if your mind is focused on your goals and is trained to achieve those goals then your subconscious mind will also be focused on those goals and will attract the situations and opportunities for you to achieve the success you want. It's really that simple.

The minute you get distracted for a prolonged period - you lose sight of your objective and fail to accomplish those goals. In order for to enjoy success - the mind has to be regularly focused on your goals - you can't stay focused for short bursts and expect to get results.

Think of it this way, your riding in a car driven by your personal driver and every time your driver asks you where you want to go you simply say: "I don't know. Wherever you want to go is fine with me." Then when your driver takes you to the place of his choice you complain and say: "I don't want to be here, take me somewhere else." And again you say you don't know where you want to go.

Can you see the confusion you would create? Can you see how you would never get to where you want to go because you haven't trained your driver to automatically take you where you want to go? You haven't given him the proper instructions.

Your mind and subconscious mind work the same way. If you don't train your mind to focus on your goals then your subconscious mind cannot create the situations that will help you achieve those goals. When you keep changing your mind, when you are not clear on what you want - your subconscious gets confused - and you end up exactly where you don't want to be.

Let's go back to the example of your personal driver. Wouldn't it be a lot easier and more comfortable if you told your driver where you wanted to go - or even better - your driver knew where you wanted to go ahead of time? But that will only happen when you train your driver by repeatedly telling him where you want to go on a regular basis.

Your subconscious mind is your driver. Your subconscious gets its instructions from your thoughts and beliefs. Give your subconscious the right instructions and it will take you where ever you want to go in life. When your mind is focused on your goals you direct your subconscious to create opportunities for you to achieve your goals. Your responsibility is to follow up on these opportunities.

How You Can Train Your Mind
Believe it or not I get a lot of calls and emails everyday from people who want to achieve their goals but simply can't get their mind to focus on the tasks that need to be done to have the success that they want. This happens

because the mind is simply not used to focusing on your goals and following up with completing those tasks. So how do you get your mind to change? How do you train your mind?

The first step is to get the mind to stop doing what it is used to doing - or break the pattern that you've been following for so long. This will require some effort - but the reward will allow you to live the life you want and enjoy the level of success that you want.

To re-train your mind and direct your subconscious mind you start by paying more attention - so that when you see yourself getting distracted and not following up on things that you wanted to do - you take a step to break the pattern. You can break the pattern by doing something else. For example: you can start following up on what you had planned to do, you can create a list and follow up with it regularly to see if you are on track.

One thing that always works is to think about your goals every morning. As you're in bed, think about your goals and think about what you can do to achieve them during the day. If you find that you constantly say: "I don't know what do to do to achieve my goals." Then you're not looking for answers in the right place.

Take a look at what other people have done to achieve similar goals and see if you can follow the same process. For example: If you want to make more money take a look at someone else who has made a lot of money and see what they've done. Can you follow their process? Maybe you can even talk to them about the process? If you want to meet someone and be in a healthy relationship, talk to a friend who is in a successful relationship and find out what they did. By doing the above exercises you train your mind to focus on finding solutions while at the same time you direct your subconscious mind to create the opportunities for you to succeed. And - you begin to create a new pattern of thinking and you start to train the mind to work differently. You're now telling your driver where you want to go. This eliminates the confusion and allows you to achieve your goals.

You're not going to magically get your mind to focus or concentrate without you taking some form of action. When you finally do take some action your mind will still resist - but as you continue taking action the resistance will subside - REPITITION. So what action can you take? First start with the exercise I just outlined above. Next - meditate. Meditation is one of the best ways to relax and calm your mind while training it to focus on what you want. When you meditate you actually start to clear the clutter that dominates your mind.

Make the Time
Finally it seems a lot of people have come to believe that they just don't have the time to achieve their goals. If you are one of the many who have such a belief then you've really convinced yourself that your goals are not worthy of your time; because if they were you would make the time for them. I'm not talking about spending an entire day or even a few hours. It's only a few minutes at different intervals. Why try to get everything crammed into one hour? Why not try to think about your goals at different intervals during the day? For example: you may have a few minutes while you're taking a walk - think of your achieving your goals. You could also do this while you're taking a shower, driving, walking, anytime. Here's a suggestion; the next time you are driving or taking a

shower, pay attention to your thoughts. Are these thoughts actually working for your or against you? Would it be better to focus on your goals or keep recycling the negative clutter or junk in your head? The choice is yours - and taking action is really about taking a small step. You don't need to spend hours meditating. Even if you simply mediated for 5 or 10 minutes a day you'd be able to increase your ability to concentrate and focus by a 100-percent within a matter of days! Do it for weeks or months and you'll have dramatic results!

How to Put Your Mind to Sleep Quickly and Rest Completely

If you often lay awake, unable to put your mind to rest while you're tossing and turning, you're going to love what you're about to read, because I'm about to share with you one of the most powerful methods for quickly shutting off your mind, and drifting off to sleep.

As you may already know, your mind must be in the Alpha brain-wave stage to fall asleep. This is the stage your mind enters you're still conscious, but your body and begin to relax. It enables your more rampant and conscious mind to turn off as you enter the realm of sleep. We all know how it feels... when you're lying awake in bed trying to fall asleep, it seems like your mind is running on hyper-speed. It's almost like you're thinking 10 times faster than when you're just normally awake and alert. In fact, if you experience this often, I can tell you for a fact that your mind IS working harder than it is when you're not trying to fall asleep, and there is a very good reason for it, here's why this happens. In my books and articles on sleep, I often teach a principle: "What you focus on expands." You see, your mind responds to

39

focus, and it goes hand in hand with the law of momentum. What is the law of momentum? Quite simply:

"Energy in motion, tends to STAY in motion"

"Energy stopped, tends to STAY stopped"

In other words, if you take action in your life, and begin to create success, you will experience more and more success every day. Success breeds success. On the other hand, if you sit your butt down on the couch to watch TV and say, "Aww, just one show, I'll only watch one show," very soon you'll be sitting there for four hours, and you'll watch five or six shows.

The law of momentum is everywhere in life, in physics, with your body, and most importantly, with your "thoughts." You see, your thinking is very predictable; it all works on the law of focus and momentum. Your mind is like a big ball of potential thinking energy, just waiting for you to give it a direction to think wildly into. It awaits and responds your every command. It's an exceptional tool except, most of us aren't very experienced at "controlling" this amazing tool. In fact, a lot people aren't even aware that they can control it! And this is where sleep problems come in.

Imagine your mind like a giant overflowing lake that's just waiting for an outlet to pour into... Slowly, when it finds an outlet, it begins with a trickle of water. That trickle turns into a stream. Then, that stream turns into a small river. Pretty soon, the small river is a giant unstoppable waterfall. Your thoughts work in the same way when you're "trying" to fall asleep.

For example, you're lying in bed, frustrated, forcing your mind to not think. "I just want to get some sleep! Stop thinking! Okay, starting now... I won't think anymore. No think... nothing. My life is nothing... If only I would finally get motivated in my job maybe I would finally create the income to start traveling instead of dealing with these problems. Problems, how can I... Ahh, I'm thinking again! Stop it!"

You get even more frustrated, and repeat the process over again in a few minutes. So how do you stop it? It's easy, you see, you can easily control your thinking, except most people aren't aware of the tools necessary! The good news is, I'm about to give you the 3-step handbook to controlling your mind. Here are the 3-universal steps that will enable you to not only stop thinking; you'll also be able to lower your brain-waves into the alpha brain-state, which will quickly let you enter sleep...

Awareness
The first step to changing anything is becoming aware that it's happening, especially if it's your mind. Pretend your mind is racing, and you finally realize that you're thinking... Most people at this stage get extremely frustrated and "try" to force the mind into submission. It doesn't work! Why? Because, what you focus on expands. The more frustrated you get, the more you're focusing on frustration, so you'll get even MORE frustration and more thinking... on and on!

So the first step is to simply become "aware" of the fact that you're thinking. Nothing more. When you notice that you're thinking, smile to yourself, and say, "I just noticed myself thinking... Interesting..." Now notice what happens inside of you when you do this... something

41

VERY profound. If "I" just noticed "myself" thinking, perhaps there are really two completely separate identities running your life? There is the "I" and there is the "self."

The "I", is the real you, the higher being, the "I" behind the mind, that runs the show, the heart, the soul, the true conscious being, the choice maker.

The "self" is the mind; if left to run the show, it will run in endless circles until the edge of insanity.

The moment you do this, the moment you become "aware" - you are no longer a slave to your mind. You have won. After you become aware... do nothing, just lay there for 3 seconds and notice how it feels to be present in who you really are, not the mind, but you, the "I" - there is a great feeling of peace behind that presence in the "I." Why? Because when you are aware like this, you're aware of the power of your choice making. You now have the power of choice.

Relaxed Focus
"What you focus on expands." Now that you have become aware of your thinking, all you have to do is "direct" your mind into a place that will bring you into a deep, deep place of relaxation. Think about it, if before your mind will relentlessly race into any direction you give it; why not pick a direction that will give you peace and restful sleep?

But, most people don't know what that direction really is. It's really easy. If you focus on anything your body does or feels subconsciously, you will begin to become more and more realized. For example your breathing, the feeling of the pillow on your head, the sounds of nature

42

outside (unless you live in the city), the warmth of your body. These are all things that happen, yet your conscious mind doesn't think about them.

As you know, "What you focus on expands"... So what would happen if you focused on something that is happening in your "subconscious"? That's right, your conscious thinking would diminish, and your subconscious mind would begin to take over the entire process of you falling asleep! It really is that simple, and it works every-time.

The easiest one is your breathing. And I promise you if you just try this tonight, you will be shocked when you wake up in the morning: "Wow! It worked!"

Repetition
As I said, the easiest one to focus on is your breathing. In the beginning, you'll find this easier said than done. Let me walk you through it.

- Begin by taking your focus onto your breathing. Take a deep breath in. Hold it for a short while, and slowly exhale...

- Count "1"

- Breathe in again... hold it shortly, exhale slowly, and count...

- "2"

Why count? Because I guarantee you, in the very beginning, you may find it challenging to hold your focus. In fact, you'll be surprised as you may not even make it to "5" the first time. This is because your conscious ever-thinking mind will butt in and interrupt. You may randomly go off into a barrage of thoughts again. If this happens, and it very well may, what do you do?

Simply become aware, and begin focusing on your breathing again. Guess what happens? As you become aware, 2 or 3 times... your mind will give up. I guarantee you, beyond the shadow of a doubt, when you get to "10" or "15" breaths you will feel a wave of relaxation in your body. This is the silent "click" as your mind shifts from the high frequency Beta brain-waves into Alpha brain-waves. Your subconscious mind will do the rest!

The following exercise will teach you how to see and recognize things that are unworthy of attention, but still recognize that they are there. In other words, attention will be paid to it and then discarded. A filter makes you totally oblivious (no attention given to it at all) that the stimuli are there and if asked to describe the situation, the filter will cause you to omit it.

*****

This chapter is the most important chapter in the book. It defines and teaches you about your mind and why you do the things you do.

But it also teaches you how to change the subconscious mind where all action/behavior/conduct occurs.

Study this chapter over and over again until it becomes set in your mind and you understand fully what it is teaching you. If you have any questions please feel free to write to me because I want you to get it right the first time.

Changing your behavior is not as easy as it sounds but it can be done. Think back and try to remember how you acquired as a belief system some of the things you do. If you learned the abhorrent behavior then you can unlearn them to and replace them with corrective behavior and conduct worthy of a peaceful existence.

Chapter 2 – Type 1 & Type 2 Con Men & The Psychology of Lying

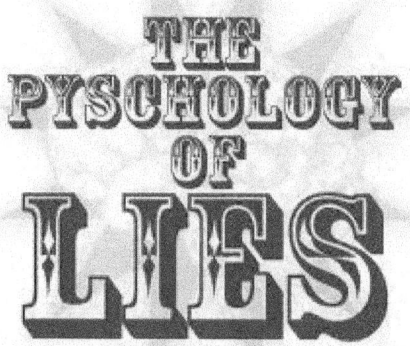

Okay, hopefully Chapter 1 opened your mind up to learning about the human behavior of both Type 1 and Type 2 con men.

Each type has different human behavioral traits yet shares some common traits too. I will describe both in detail in this chapter. I will also get into the psychology of lying and why this is the most important trait of a con man.

Type 1 Con Men

Diabolical is defined as: "of, relating to, or characteristic of the devil: devilish <a *diabolical* plot>"

and is one of the best descriptions of a con man to date.

Com men are VERY diabolical and enjoy what they do. Their actions and conduct are purposeful and deliberate and they know full well of what they are doing. They cannot hide behind some psychological disorder or claim some childhood trauma made them practice their deceptive trade.

In a court of law, they are doomed because they have no defense whatsoever. This is apparent with some of the court cases that have been reported in the media recently. Bernie Madoff received a 150 year sentence for his decades of deception and his actions left a good many people scratching their heads in wonder including his wife and family as well as the regulators and law enforcement.

Bernie Madoff knew full well what he was doing was a massive con game and lived within this game for decades even deceiving himself that he could continue it forever. Unfortunately the economy fell out and exposed him as well as numerous other con men of a lesser degree of fame and fortune.

Here is a list of Type 1 Con Men, some of whom you know and can identify but others you have never seen before:

The 10-Most Famous Con Men in History

1. Frank Abagnale [Born: 1948]

Frank Abagnale is a former cheque con artist, forger and imposter who, for five years in the 1960s, passed bad checks worth more than $2.5 million in 26 countries. The recent blockbuster film Catch Me If You Can is based on his life. His first experience of fraud was as a youth when he used his father's Mobil card to buy car parts that he would then sell back to the gas station for a lower price. He did not realize that his father was the one who had to foot the bill and when he was eventually confronted with the fraud, his mother sent him for four months to a juvenile correction facility.

After moving to New York, Frank lived solely on the income of his fraudulent activities. One of his most famous tricks was to print his own account number on fake bank deposit slips so that when clients of the bank deposited money, it would actually go in to his account. By the time the banks realized what had happened, Frank had taken $40,000 and run.

For two years, Abagnale travelled around the world free by masquerading as a Pan Am pilot. He was able to abuse the professional courtesy of other airlines to provide free transport for competing airline pilots if they had to move to another city at short notice. When he was nearly caught leaving a plane, he changed his masquerade to that of a Doctor. He worked as a medical supervisor for 11 months without detection. At other times he worked as a lawyer and a teacher.

He was eventually caught in France and spent six months in prison there. After that he was extradited to Sweden and imprisoned for a further six months. After a successful escape whilst travelling to the United States, he was finally given 12 years in Prison. He escaped from his prison by masquerading as an undercover officer of the Bureau of Prisons. He was once again captured in New York City and returned to jail. After serving only five years of his sentence, the US Federal Government offered him his freedom in return for helping the government against fraud and scam artists without pay.

He currently runs Abagnale and Associates, a financial fraud consultancy company and is a multi-millionaire.

2. Charles Ponzi [Born: 1882; Died: 1949]

Ponzi, an Italian immigrant to the United States became one of the most famous con men in American history. While many people do not know the name Ponzi, the Ponzi Scheme is extremely well known and continues today in Internet Make Money Fast schemes. His early life is not entirely known as he was prone to fabricate stories about it. What is known is that he spent a short amount of time at University in Rome and, after dropping out, caught a boat to Boston, USA where he arrived with $2.50 in his pocket.

His early years in the United States were troublesome. He began working at a restaurant but was soon fired for playing tricks with the bills and shortchanging customers. His next job was working in a bank in Canada that catered to Italian immigrants. His knowledge of numbers helped him to do very well there. Unfortunately it turned out that the owner of the bank was stealing money from newly opened savings accounts to pay the interest on the interest bearing accounts and to cover bad investments. The bank owner eventually fled to Mexico and left Ponzi without a job. After writing a fraudulent cheque and spending a number of years in prison, Ponzi determined to become wealthy at any cost.

Once he had settled in to life on the outside, he discovered postal reply coupons through a letter that was sent to him from abroad. He realized that he could buy foreign coupons at massively devalued prices (because of price fixing after the war) and then resell them in the United States for a 400% profit. This was a form of arbitrage and it was legal. Ponzi began canvasses friends and acquaintances for money – promising them a 50% return or a doubling of their money in 90 days. He started his own company, the Securities Exchange Company, to promote the scheme.

The word of this great investment quickly spread and before long Ponzi was living in a luxurious mansion. He was bringing in cash at a fantastic rate, but the simplest financial analysis showed that he wasn't making money, he was losing it rapidly. For every dollar he took in, he went more deeply into debt. As long as money kept flowing in, Ponzi would stay ahead of the eventual collapse.

People soon began to become suspicious and the press was starting to publish negative articles about him. Inevitably people were starting to demand their money. Shortly after, federal agents raided his office and shut it down. No stock of stamps was found and everyone that had invested their money with Ponzi lost every penny. It is probably that he lost tens of millions of dollars. Ponzi plead guilty of mail fraud and was sent to prison. After one escape he was returned to jail to complete his sentence. He was eventually deported back to Italy and he died there in poverty in 1949.

3. Joseph Weil [Born: 1877; Died: 1975]

Joseph "Yellow Kid" Weil was one of the most famous con men in his era. Over the course of his career he is believed to have stolen over 8 million dollars. In his first job as a collector, he realized that his co-workers were collecting their debts but keeping a little part of the money for themselves. Weil started a protection racket – offering not to report their activities in return for a small portion of what they were taking.

He also used phony oil deals, women, fixed races, and an endless list of other tricks to steal from an increasingly gullible public. He could change his persona daily to further his gains: one day he was Dr. Henri Reuel, a noted geologist who travelled around and told his hosts that he was a representative for a big oil company while draining them of the cash they gave him to "invest in fuel." The next day he was director of the Elysium Development Company, promising land to innocent believers while robbing them in recording and abstract

51

fees. Or he was a chemist par excellence, who had discovered how to copy dollar bills; promising to increase your fortune, he would multiply your bills then take the booty once the police arrived.

In his autobiography, Weil writes:

"The desire to get something for nothing has been very costly to many people who have dealt with me and with other con men," Weil writes. "But I have found that this is the way it works. **The average person, in my estimation, is ninety-nine per cent animal and one per cent human.** The ninety-nine per cent that is animal causes very little trouble. But the one per cent that is human causes all our woes. When people learn — as I doubt they will — that they can't get something for nothing, crime will diminish and we shall live in greater harmony."

4. Victor Lustig [Born: 1890; Died: 1947]

Victor Lustig was renowned as the Man who Sold the Eiffel Tower. He was born in Bohemia but later moved to Paris where he was able to con people on his frequent journeys between Paris and New York. His first con was to show people a device that could print $100 bills. The only problem, he would tell them, is that it only prints one bill every six hours. Many people paid him enormous amounts of money (usually over $30,000) for the device. In fact, the device contained two real hidden $100 bills – once they were spat out by the machine it would produce only blank paper. By the time the buyers discovered this, Lustig was well gone with their money.

In 1925, as France was recovering from the war, the upkeep of the Eiffel tower was an almost unbearable expense for the city of Paris. When Lustig read about this in a paper, he came up with his most brilliant idea. After forging government credentials, he invited six scrap metal dealers to a secret meeting in a hotel. He explained that the City could not afford to keep the tower and that they had to sell it for scrap. He told them the secrecy of the meeting and all future dealings was due to the fact that the public may become distressed at the idea of the removal of the tower.

While it seems implausible, at the time the tower was built it was meant to be temporary and this happened just 18 years after the original date for removal of the tower. Lustig took the dealers in a limousine to tour the tower. One of the dealers, Andre Poisson was convinced that the tale was legitimate and he handed over the money. When he realized he had been conned, he was too embarrassed to tell the police and Lustig escaped with the money. One month later, he returned to Paris to try the whole scam again. This time it was reported to the police but Lustig managed to escape.

At one point, Lustig convinced Al Capone to invest $50,000 with him. He stored the money in a vault and returned it two months later, stating that the deal had fallen through. Capone, so impressed by Lustig's honesty gave him $5,000 for his effort. In 1934, Lustig was found guilty of counterfeiting. He pled guilty and was sentenced to 20 years in Alcatraz. In 1947 he died of pneumonia whilst in jail in Springfield, Missouri.

5. George Parker [Born: 1870; Died: 1936]

Parker was one of the most audacious con men in American history. He made his living selling New York's public landmarks to unwary tourists. His favorite object for sale was the Brooklyn Bridge, which he sold twice a week for years. He convinced his marks that they could make a fortune by controlling access to the roadway. More than once police had to remove naive buyers from the bridge as they tried to erect toll barriers.

Other public landmarks he sold included the original Madison Square Garden, the Metropolitan Museum of Art, Grant's Tomb, and the Statue of Liberty. George had many different methods for making his sales. When he sold Grant's Tomb, he would often pose as the general's grandson. He even set up a fake "office" to handle his real estate swindles. He produced impressive forged documents to prove that he was the legal owner of whatever property he was selling.

Parker was convicted of fraud three times. After his third conviction on December 17th, 1928 he was sentenced to a life term at Sing Sing Prison. He spent the last eight years of his life behind bars. He was popular among guards and fellow inmates who enjoyed hearing of his exploits. George is remembered as one of the most successful con men in the history of the United States, as well as one of history's most talented hoaxers. His exploits have passed into popular culture, giving rise to phrases such as "and if you believe that, I have a bridge to sell you", a popular way of expressing a belief that someone is gullible.

6. Soapy Smith [Born: 1860; Died: 1898]

Soapy Smith (born Jefferson Randolph Smith) was an American con artist and gangster who had a major hand in the organized criminal operations of Denver, Colorado, Creede, Colorado, and Skagway, Alaska from 1879 to 1898. He is perhaps the most famous "sure-thing" bunko man of the old west. Sometime in the late 1870s or early 1880s, Smith began duping entire crowds with a ploy the Denver newspapers dubbed The Prize Package Soap Sell Swindle.

Jefferson would open his "tripe and keister" (display case on a tripod) on a busy street corner. Piling ordinary soap cakes onto the keister top, he would describe their wonders. As he spoke to the growing crowd of curious onlookers, he would pull out his wallet and begin wrapping paper money ranging from one dollar up to one hundred dollars, around a select few of the bars. He then finished each bar by wrapping plain paper around it to hide the money. He mixed the money-wrapped packages in with wrapped bars containing no money. He then sold the soap to the crowd for a dollar a cake.

A shill planted in the crowd would buy a bar, tear it open it, and loudly proclaim that he had won some money, waving it around for all to see. This performance had the desired effect of enticing the sale of the packages. More often than not, victims bought several bars before the sale was completed. Midway through the sale, Smith would announce that the hundred-dollar bill still remained in the pile, unpurchased. He then would auction off the remaining soap bars to the highest bidders.

Through the masterful art of manipulation and sleight-of-hand, the cakes of soap wrapped with money were hidden and replaced with packages holding no cash. It was assured that the only money "won" went to members of what became known as the "Soap Gang." Soapy was eventually shot to death by a group he swindled in a card game.

7. Eduardo de Valfierno

Eduardo de Valfierno, who referred to himself as Marqués (marquis), was an Argentine con man who allegedly masterminded the theft of the Mona Lisa. Valfierno paid several men to steal the work of art from the Louvre, including museum employee Vincenzo Peruggia. On August 21, 1911 Peruggia hid the Mona Lisa under his coat and simply walked out the door.

Before the heist took place, Valfierno commissioned French art restorer and forger Yves Chaudron to make six copies of the Mona Lisa. The forgeries were then shipped to various parts of the world, readying them for the buyers he had lined up. Valfierno knew once the Mona Lisa was stolen it would be harder to smuggle copies past customs. After the heist the copies were delivered to their buyers, each thinking they had the original which had just been stolen for them. Because Valfierno just wanted to sell forgeries, he only needed the original Mona Lisa to disappear and never contacted Peruggia again after the crime. Eventually Peruggia was caught trying to sell the painting and it was returned to the Louvre in 1913.

8. James Hogue [Born: 1959]

Hogue is a US impostor who most famously entered Princeton University by posing as a self-taught orphan. In 1986 Hogue enrolled in a Palo Alto High School as Jay Mitchell Huntsman, a 16-year-old orphan from Nevada. He had adopted the identity of a dead infant. A suspicious local reporter exposed him. In 1988 Hogue enrolled at Princeton University using the alias Alexi Indris Santana, a self-taught orphan from Utah. He deferred admission for one year because he had been convicted of the theft of bicycle frames in Utah. Hogue claimed in his application materials that he had slept outside in the Grand Canyon, raising sheep and reading philosophers. He violated his parole to enter class. For the next two years he lived as Santana and as a member of the track team. He was also admitted into the Ivy Club.

In 1991 Hogue's real identity was exposed when Renee Pacheco, a student from the Palo Alto High School, recognized him. He was arrested for defrauding the university for $30,000 in financial aid and sentenced to three years in jail with 5-years probation and 100 hours of community service.

On May 16, 1993 Hogue made headlines again through his association with Harvard University. Having lied about his identity again, he was able to take a job as a security guard in one of Harvard's on campus museums. A few months into his tenure, museum officials noticed that several gemstones on exhibit had been replaced with inexpensive fakes. Somerville police seized Hogue in his home and charged him with grand larceny to the tune of $50,000.

On March 12, 2007 Hogue pleaded guilty to a single felony count of theft of more than $15,000 in exchange for a prison sentence not to exceed 10 years, and prosecutors' agreement to drop other theft and habitual criminal charges.

9. Robert Hendy-Freegard [Born: 1971]

Robert Hendy-Freegard is a British barman, car salesman, conman and impostor who masqueraded as an MI5 agent and fooled several people to go underground for fear of IRA assassination. He met his victims on social occasions or as customers in the pub or car dealership where he was working. He would reveal his "role" as an undercover agent for MI5, Special Branch or Scotland Yard working against the IRA. He would win them over, ask for money and make them do his bidding. He demanded that they cut off contact with family and friends, go through "loyalty tests" and live alone in poor conditions. He seduced five women, claiming that he wanted to marry them. Initially some of the victims refused to co-operate with the police because he had warned them that police would be double agents or MI5 agents performing another "loyalty test".

Hendy-Freegard also seduced a newly married personal assistant who was taking care of his children. He told her he was with MI5 and forced her to cut contact with friends and family lest the IRA would kill her. He also took naked pictures of her and threatened to give them to her husband if she would not cooperate. She had to change her name and tell the deed poll officer it was because she was sexually abused as a child. Her loyalty tests included sleeping in Heathrow airport and on park benches for several nights and pretending to be a Jehovah's Witness so that his bosses in MI5 would let them marry.

In 2002 Scotland Yard and the FBI organized a sting operation. First, the FBI bugged the phone of the American psychologist's parents. Her mother told Hendy-Freegard she would hand over £10,000 but only in person. Hendy-Freegard met the mother in Heathrow airport where police apprehended him. He denied all charges and claimed they were part of a conspiracy against him and continued this story in the subsequent trial. On June 23, 2005, after an eight month trial, Blackfriars Crown Court convicted Robert Hendy-Freegard for two counts of kidnapping, 10 of theft and 8 of deception. On September 6, 2005 he was given a life sentence. Police doubt that they have discovered all the victims. On April 25, 2007, the BBC reported that Robert Hendy-Freegard had appealed against his kidnapping convictions and won. This means that the life sentence is revoked but he will still serve nine years for the other offences. He could be free by the end of 2007.

10. Bernard Cornfeld [Born: 1927; Died: 1995]

Bernard Cornfeld was a prominent businessman and international financier who sold investments in US mutual funds. He was born in Turkey. When he moved to the US, he first worked as a social worker but became a mutual fund salesman in the 1950s. Although he suffered from a stammer, he had a natural gift for selling and when a schoolfriend's father died, the two of them used the $3,000 insurance money to purchase and run an age and weight guessing stand at the Coney Island funfair.

In the 1960s, Cornfeld formed his own mutual fund selling company, Investors Overseas Services (IOS), which he incorporated outside the US with funds in Canada and headquarters in Geneva, Switzerland. Although the headquarters were officially in Geneva, the main operational offices of IOS were in Ferney-Voltaire, France, a short drive from the Swiss border to Geneva— this was simply a means of avoiding the problems of obtaining Swiss work-permits for the many employees. During the next ten years, IOS raised in excess of $2.5 billion, bringing Cornfeld a personal fortune of more than $100 million. Cornfeld himself became known for conspicuous consumption with lavish parties. Socially, he was generous and jovial.

A group of 300 IOS employees complained to the Swiss authorities that Cornfeld and his co-founders pocketed part of the proceeds of a share issue raised among employees in 1969. Consequently he was charged with fraud in 1973 by the Swiss authorities. When Cornfeld visited Geneva, Swiss authorities arrested him. He served 11 months in a Swiss jail before being freed on a bail surety of $600,000. He returned to Beverly Hills, living less ostentatiously than in his previous years. He developed an obsession for health foods and vitamins, renounced red meat and seldom drank alcohol. He suffered a stroke and died of a cerebral aneurysm on 27th February 1995 in London, England.

Con Men Living Today

- **Frank Abagnale** (1948): U.S. check forger and impostor; his autobiography was made into the movie *Catch Me If You Can*.
- **Sergio Cragnotti** (1940): Former Italian industrialist and president of a football team who masterminded the Cirio bankruptcy.
- **Marc Dreier** (1950): Founder of attorney firm Dreier LLP. Convicted of selling approximately $700 million worth of fictitious promissory notes, and other crimes.
- **Kevin Foster** (1958/59): British investment fraudster, convicted of running a Ponzi scheme.
- **Robert Hendy-Freegard** (1971): Briton who kidnapped people by impersonating an MI5 agent and conned them out of money.
- **James Arthur Hogue** (1959): U.S. impostor who most famously entered Princeton University by posing as a self-taught orphan
- **Sante Kimes:** Convicted of fraud, robbery, murder, and over 100 other crimes
- **Matt the Knife** (1981): American-born con artist, card cheat and pickpocket who, from the ages of approximately 14 through 21, bilked dozens of casinos, corporations and at least one Mafia crime family.
- **Steven Kunes** (1956): Former television screenwriter with convictions for forgery, grand

theft, and false use of financial information. In 1982 he attempted to sell a faked interview with J. D. Salinger to *People* magazine.

- **Bernard Madoff** (1938): Former American stock broker and non-executive chairman of the NASDAQ stock market who admitted to the operation of the largest Ponzi scheme in history.
- **Barry Minkow** (1967): Known for the *ZZZZ Best* scam.
- **Richard Allen Minsky** (1944): Scammed female victims for sex by pretending to be jailed family members over the phone.
- **Lou Pearlman** (1954): Former boy band impresario, convicted for perpetrating a large and long-running Ponzi scheme.
- Steven Jay Russell (1957): Georgia deputy police officer who impersonated several individuals to escape from a Texas prison, and embezzled over hundreds of thousands of dollars from the North American Medical Management corporation. Best known for pretending to be dying from AIDS in order to transfer out of prison, only to be caught after later trying to appeal his life-partner Phillip Morris' jail sentence. Inspired a movie titled: "I Love You Phillip Morris"
- **Calisto Tanzi** (1938): Former Italian industrialist and president of Parmalat, which he led to one of the costliest bankruptcies in history.
- **Kevin Trudeau** (1963): US writer and billiards promoter, convicted of fraud and larceny, known for late-night infomercials and books about "Natural Cures 'They' Don't Want You to Know About".

*****

One important factor to remember when it comes to Type 1 con men is that all of their actions are deliberate and purposeful. They all know they are conning people and they all know that they are in it for pecuniary gain.

The criminal mind has convinced itself that getting something for nothing is better than getting it in a lawful manner.

Con men believe that they are superior to other people, and that others simply don't have the intelligence to catch them. They have no empathy or compassion for anything.

In studies conducted by my Applied Mind Sciences lab using captured and imprisoned con men we did discover that 6 out of 10 con men have a very high intelligence quotient (IQ). The other 4 had average intelligence and all four claimed that they got into the con game by accident and were trying to make things right before they got caught. Interesting ,eh? Remorse is a funny thing; remorse comes after a person is caught but never comes up during the con game.

The fact of the matter is that the majority of con men view other people as sheep to be herded and conned. They have no regard whatsoever of the damage they do and the lives they ruin and they simply do not care. Why they do this will be discussed in more detail in Chapter 3.

Now let's discuss Type 2 individuals…

Type 2 Individuals

I call Type 2 people "individuals" rather than con men for the simple fact that many Type 2 individuals are not purposeful in their actions to committing a crime. The ARE purposeful in their actions to manipulate but not insofar as for the purpose of pecuniary gain in any form.

Type 2 individuals are manipulators and some are very good at it and practice it daily. There manipulators can be anyone from your mommy, other family members, friends, co-workers and more.

They hide their actions behind the facade of only "trying to help" when in reality, they are "only trying to harm."

They are not diabolical but they are immature and hurtful in their actions. The reasons behind their actions are as varied as the individuals themselves and depending on the relationship; the reasons can be jealousy, hate, envy, revenge, enjoyment in hurting others, and wanting to bring others down to their level, and more...

Like I stated in my introduction, chances are that you may never come in contact with a Type 1 con man, but you do come in contact with Type 2 individuals daily and this is why I consider Type 2 individuals more dangerous.

The fact of the matter is that with the advent of the Internet and having information at your fingertips, people allow others to do their thinking.

I had a staff manager and co-worker years ago that was a master manipulator and always used the saying, "I didn't hire you to think; I will do your thinking for you." When I pointed out that this was not the way to manage my people, her response was, "It works for me and I have managed this way for years."

Candidly, I was dumbfounded by her response and just looked at her before I replied, "What has worked for you? You have been married three times, your kids don't even talk to you, you have the highest employee turnover in the company and I can bet even your dog hates your guts."

She then stated emphatically that I could not talk to her in that manner and stormed away so I fired her. She then filed a lawsuit against me and the company, which she lost horribly and to this day, has never been hired by another company in a managerial position.

In essence, this woman was deceiving herself and self-deception is the worst form of deception.

The Psychology of Lying

One of the most perplexing human conditions is why people find a need to lie, cheat and deceive. Deception has become a lifestyle and more people spend their lives within a web of deception than outside of it. They have built whole worlds within their existences and many have no idea how it occurred or how to stop it.

In this book, I want to address the subject of lies, cheats and deception in detail and I am quite certain you will be amazed. One would think that les, cheating and deception are really one-in-the-same but they are not and like I said, you will be amazed at just how distinct the reasons behind all three really are and how compelling they are to break.

In the book, "Man Up-The Decline & Fall of Manhood" Dr. Noah Pranksky defines the decline of manhood with the main cause being deception.

http://www.amazon.com/dp/B006JA2UMG

Furthermore, in another of his books, "Female Wolf Packs" he demonstrates the problems men have with women and the leading problem is deception.

http://www.amazon.com/dp/B006JMHD80

The problem of "trust' between genders has become so severe that each gender is literally giving up on relationships and going off to form family units without the opposite gender in the picture. Women are using the services of sperm banks to sire children and men are choosing surrogate mothers.

The question of "why" has been a part of the conscience of man since the dawn of time. It has caused us to seek answers, better solutions, invention, progress, increased knowledge and more.

But more often than not, most of our questions of "why" now centers on personal behavioral traits and habits that perplex us and cause us consternation and regret.

Candidly, most people have no idea why they do the things they do so in this book I am going to explain in detail why you lie, cheat and deceive and how to overcome these perplexing problems.

Me, I'm dishonest, and you can always trust a dishonest man to be dishonest. Honestly, it's the honest ones you have to watch out for.
Johnny Depp

Where is the gain for people who lie, cheat and deceive? This is an important question to ask too.

In Chapter 1, I explained the difference between true reality that the conscious mind SEES and the PERCEIVED reality that the subconscious mind uses. There is a difference and the difference is quite large.

A liar, cheater and deceiver does perceive a big gain in their behavior, otherwise they would not do what they do. This perception is a wrongful belief system and hence; their gain is a false gain.

But candidly, even a false gain is worthy of their actions even if this appears silly on the surface. In essence the very first person they deceive is themselves.

In my book, "The Greatest Fraud The World Has Ever Known," I go to the root of the problem of self deception.

http://www.amazon.com/dp/B008GUBKI2

"The Greatest Fraud The World Has Ever Known" is the person practicing deception because they are only fooling themselves into believing that this is a lifestyle worth pursuing.

Here is an excerpt from my book…

In today's world, fraud is running rampant. But in actuality, fraud is not new concept. From the beginning of time man has used deception from everything such as war to love.

In the animal kingdom, animals use deception for protection by the use of camouflage and more.

The high technology of our times makes access to all forms of information almost instantaneous and the news media sensationalizes fraud to a point of frenzy.

Fraud is defined as intentional deception made for personal gain or to damage another individual.

In recent years, top fraudsters such as Bernie Madoff, Ken Lay and Jeff Skilling of Enron, Allen Stanford, Bernie Ebbers of Worldcom, Dennis Kozlowski of Tyco International, Martin Frankel, James Lewis, Lou Pearlman of N'Sync fame, Barry Minkow of ZZZZ Best, and Tom Petters have been brought to justice and given lengthy prison terms.

No one seemingly escapes fraud; everyone on the planet has been deceived in some manner.

As Chief Forensics Investigator for ForensicsNation.com, I compile and preserve evidence of cyber-crime fraud all the time.

Cyber crime is rampant too and growing; you would not believe how exposed the average citizen is today.

Society has come to rely on computers, cell phones, and computer-run public systems such as traffic lights, food distribution, water supply and much more in such a way that any disruption of these services jeopardizes our quality of life.

People make use of Wi-Fi systems inside their homes, in public places such as libraries and Starbucks, which make them huge targets for hackers and crackers.

As a behavioral scientist, I have studied the criminal mind and have made many conclusions.

Recently we busted a voyeur using a wireless camera to spy on a Hooters waitress while she was undressing in her apartment. We caught him a couple of blocks away in his car with a handheld viewing device.

When I played back what he had seen for the waitress, her comment was, "Why? He could see more on the Internet."

And yes, it is true, you can Google just about any body part you want and see more on the Internet but the waitress missed the one important factor that causes crime - the thrill of getting away with something that is forbidden!

When a person thinks of fraud, rarely do they ever think along the lines of defrauding themselves but yet this is the most common occurrences of fraud.

Self deception runs rampant in our respective psyches; the ability to deceive ourselves cannot be minimized.

This book addresses this self deception and our inherent need to defraud ourselves.

We defraud ourselves in many ways; too many to list here but here is a partial list: the way we eat, how much we eat, our diets in general, our looks, our need to be loved, sex, our need to achieve, our beliefs, and more.

The total essences of our lives are completely affected by self deception; most of our personal existences cannot be lived without the deceptions we have created.

Let me give you an example: A person buys an automobile that they really cannot afford because it provides a status symbol of success. In many people's minds, a high-priced automobile means they "made it" but the reality is they haven't made it at all unless you count making themselves a slave to the monthly bill that pays for the automobile.

The reality of the high monthly payment takes a back seat to the perception of the automobile being a status symbol.

People overeat to assuage some pain due to stress and anxiety. They deceive themselves into believing that eating takes their minds off their problems.

They lie, gossip and deceive because it brings others that they perceive are above them down to their level.

This is the main cause of bullying and malicious gossip. We all do it; maybe not to a point where something really bad occurs like suicide, but we all still do it.

Without a doubt, we deceive ourselves the most when it comes to looks and beauty. Everything from anorexia to tanning to the clothes we wear top the list of self deception due to concerns over how a person looks.

Why are physical things leading the list of self deceptions? Why aren't the mental things at the top? After all, all of our self deceptions originate in the subconscious mind.

In this book, I will attempt to answer these questions and more. I will examine our need for self deception and the results of practicing this interesting human trait.

I will offer examples for you to ponder and that will demonstrate the core essential of my premises. None of what I present must be taken as a given; deception is subjective, which means it becomes anything you want it to become.

What is objective here is studying my core essential premises and weighing them against your own existence. A thorough and object examination of yourself may become painful but you will quickly realize that your own self deceptions rob you of a quiet and peaceful existence.

One objective fact is quite persistent throughout this book - The Greatest Fraud the World Has Ever Known is YOU!

Self-Deception is rampant and it isn't going to go away as long as the person practicing it perceives it as something of value.

It is quite easy to deceive yourself and a person can rationalize this deception in so many ways that it literally boggles the mind. Even with the facts known and presented to the person, the urge and need to keep the deception going is huge.

Let me give you an example…

Recently on Amazon.com I was personally attacked in the Amazon forum by a "gang" of people that had appointed themselves as Amazon Review Cops. They were harassing authors claiming that their reviews of their books were faked and they were paid reviews. They went on to accuse me as being a "paid reviewer" because I write a good many reviews.

No amount of reasoning appeased these people so I reported them to Amazon along with a plethora of authors that they had also attacked. I then filed criminal stalking charges and a federal district lawsuit for damages.

You should have heard the howl and the cry from this gang of people. They wrote to Amazon to complain that I had targeted them and were being unfair filing criminal charges and a civil lawsuit.

Amazon's response was to tell them not to harass authors with unfounded accusations or in other words…tough, you are on your own.

Now, this gang perceived they were doing good when all they were doing was putting on a false front for what they really wanted to do, which was harass authors. They cared nothing about the reviews; they only wanted the authors to engage them in the forum where this gang could literally "tear them apart' and ruin their brand and reputation.

What they didn't expect was ME! This "homey" don't play no games and this gang never even considered the consequences of an author fighting back. It was so shocking to them that the majority of the gang wrote to me apologizing for their actions and asking to be removed from the suit. My response: "NO WAY!" Each gang member is accountable for their actions and they will pay the price for ruining brands and reputations. BTW – I had given them fair warning that if they continued in their behavior that I would file a criminal complaint and civil lawsuit; they just didn't believe it.

Here is my point and it is a big one: a person IS ALWAYS accountable for their actions and even if you deceive yourself into believing that your actions are justified then be prepared to defend yourself in a court of law. You are not invisible on the Internet.

Chapter 3 – Living In a Fantasy World

Now I want to identify the main cause and reason behind con men and manipulators. It is living a fantasy life as if it were real.

In my best-selling book, "Fantasy is Easy-Everything Is Perfect, Behavioral science looks at people who live their lives within a fantasy" http://www.amazon.com/dp/B00BFF81CS I outline in detail how a fantasy life destroys a person's existence.

It is a known fact within the research confines of behavioral science that the human subconscious mind cannot tell the difference between fantasy and reality. For example: your conscious mind knows that you are sitting in a movie theater watching a movie but your subconscious mind does not and when a sad scene comers along, you respond with the same emotions as if the scene was real…maybe you cry, get angry, or simply melancholy.

There has been as good many news stories recently dealing with people that have committed horrible crimes – Sandy Hook Elementary School, Aurora, CO Movie Theater killings, etc – and the questions usually raised first deal with violent video games, and the things that may have influenced behavior or cause these acts of violence. Is this true? We shall see…

Is Fantasy a Bad Thing?

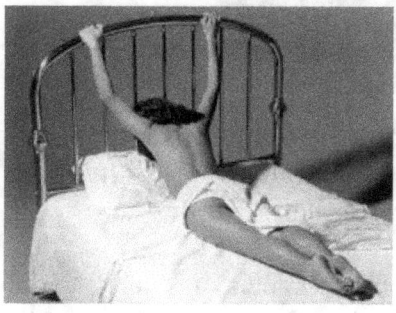

I have been a behavioral scientist for over 32-years and I am the Chief Research Scientist at Applied Mind Sciences and the question I am asked the most is this: "Is Fantasy a Bad Thing?"

So here is my answer and listen closely because it is a qualified answer: "There is good fantasy and there is bad fantasy but ANY fantasy whether good or bad that causes an individual to walk up and down within this fantasy and that manifests itself as outward behavior is BAD."

A good fantasy is one that causes you to grow as a person. Years ago I took ballroom dancing lessons and would picture myself on the dance floor mimicking the dance steps that my instructor taught me. This is an example of a good fantasy and believe me it is FANTASY since today I suck as a ballroom dancer (lol).

But let me give you a more poignant example. Many years ago I was assigned a patient that had been arrested in Las Vegas for impersonating a general flag officer of the US Military. The US Military had been aware of this man's actions for some time but when he showed up at Nellis Air Force Base, which is located on the outskirts of Las Vegas, they had him arrested.

This poor guy was really messed up. When I went to visit him at Clark County Detention Center, he demanded that I stand at attention and address him as "sir".

When I eventually made contact with his family, they were completely dumbfounded over his behavior. He had always been a loving husband and father, worked his job as an insurance executive for over 20-years, had never been in trouble before; not even a parking ticket. Then – WHAMO – out of the blue he pulls this stunt and is arrested.

I worked with this man for almost a year; got the charges dropped in return for him going through treatment, and I learned some extraordinary things from interviewing this man.

77

When this man was 18-years old he applied for service in the US Army but was rejected because of a perforated eardrum. He really had wanted to join the US Army and the rejection was apparently way too much for his young mind to handle so he began a "secret' fantasy of being in the US Army and he was the best soldier the world had ever seen.

In his fantasy as in all fantasies, everything is perfect. You are always the best looking person, the most admired, you are never sick or have a bad hair day, and you can do anything and everything, and so on.

In fact, after hundreds of hours of interviews with this man, if he could write a sentence he could have become one of the best action/adventure novelists on the planet; some of his stories were very exciting adventures.

It is important to note that his family knew none of this; his fantasy was truly a secret. Most people that pass you on the street daily are living their lives within some type of fantasy and their fantasies are secret too and for the most part harmless unless the fantasy begins to manifest itself in outward behavior.

So why do people do this? And even if the fantasy life of an individual does not manifest itself in outward behavior, is there any harm in living a fantasy life?

Allow me to answer the first question, "Why do people do this?" The answer is fairly obvious; they do it because, in their minds, they cannot achieve their fantasy in real life. It is also an extreme form of self-entertainment that can easily spin out of control.

In today's tough economic climate you have a plethora of situations that people feel helpless to control. College students graduating have no jobs to go to and more often than not a huge student loan debt to pay off. The American Dream has failed these young people.

Companies are downsizing and layoffs are all too common. And even as economic conditions improve, many companies have found they do not need to rehire these people that they did quite well without them.

Relationships are faltering. Young men and women are giving up on finding meaningful relationships and mates and are going off by themselves to build their lives alone.

In actuality, the list is endless and as the reasons stack up so do the fantasy lives for those who can still dream of being what they always wanted to be.

Now to the second question, "And even if the fantasy life of an individual does not manifest itself in outward behavior, is there any harm in living a fantasy life?"

The short answer is "yes" but more than likely not for the reasons you probably surmise.

Fantasy life is free; there is no effort expended, no money changes hands for training, and there is no recourse within a fantasy because everything is perfect. BUT, as the world defines, "Everything has a cost," and the cost an individual pays is that he/she gives up in reality attempting to acquire their dream/goal.

And why not? You can become anything you want in a fantasy but there are no guarantees offered in real life. And remember, fantasies are free; in real life there are costs to become anything. Time is investment, money paid in fees, tuition, books, and more.

I want to take it one step further…look at the picture under the Chapter heading above. It shows a woman tied to a bed frame. This is the result of a fantasy life that has spiraled down into the pit of depravity.

The human mind will ALWAYS seek depravity unless checked by parents, friends, the law, and social mores, etc. This why pornography is bad; if left unchecked, lust seeks a bigger and greater thrill that can lead ultimately to a serial killer or serial rapist. Step-by-step it spirals down into the pit of depravity.

In the next chapter, I am going to delve deeper into this depravity and demonstrate how erratic and violent behavior can be a result of bad fantasy.

Causes of Manifested Behavior Other Than Mental Disease

It is easy to blame mental disease for a plethora of manifested behaviors and in many cases this would be true but not always.

It makes a good defense in court but many cases claiming mental incompetence are being shot down by psychologist as being shams.

I want to now examine other causes of manifested behavior stemming from living a life within a fantasy.

I made a list and I will expand on this list as we go along…

- **Childhood Causes** – these are causes that develop within the course of a person's upbringing. It takes into account many of the factors listed below including childhood trauma, maturity, and environment. How we are raised, where we are raised and what type of an environment we are raised in all play a factor in a person's eventual adult existence.

- **Childhood Trauma** – a good many children suffer from many types of childhood traumas including physical and verbal abuse, molestation, bullying, disease, and more. These traumas can manifest themselves immediately or later on in adult life.

- **Child Rearing** – the way we are raised bears a good deal on how and what we become in our adult lives. Economic conditions have forced both parents into the workplace and children are left to themselves or day care facilities. The home environment contributes heavily to the problem especially if parents often fight because of finances, poor marital relations or whatever causes a tenuous home environment.

- **Maturity** – this is probably one of the most contributing factors to embracing a fantasy life since a person's maturity level bears a direct influence on how a person handles all situations in life. Remember, it is easy to be drawn into a fantasy life because everything in a fantasy life is perfect and free.

- **Mimicking Behavior Patterns** - A child that grows up in a home of violence tends to be violent. Parents that smoke and drink tend to raise children that exhibit the same behavior. Children will observe and mimic all types of behavior that they see their parents do as well as other adults and children. If left unchecked, these behavioral patterns can become set for life.

- **Environment** – the environment in which we are raised and live is the second most important factor contributing to the withdrawal into a fantasy life. It is easy to retreat into a world that the person deems as perfect. We tend to dream of the perfect but live in the flawed!! If we cannot change our physical environment then we can withdraw into a world that is far more satisfying than the one we actually live in.

- **Self-Entertainment** – this is a contributing factor that cannot be dismissed since I see it occurring almost daily. In the past, we called it daydreaming and it was deemed seemingly innocuous. Today, we now know that this trait is practiced by individuals far more often than first believed. It has become the scourge of the workplace as individuals withdraw into their own worlds leaving workloads untouched. Young people complain that the opposite gender only wants entertainment and fun with no commitment. Many complain that the opposite gender is in a world unto themselves and in many cases this is true.

- **Pathological Liars** – this is not a matter of low self-esteem; in fact it usually is a case of too much self-esteem. And more and more cases are being recorded where the individual lies but is not considered a pathological liar. Everybody lies;

this is a given, but the reasons behind the lie determine the extent of which a person will go to keep his fantasy life going. In this case, the fantasy life is most important. Let me give you an example: I am going to tell you a lie right now. Ready? I am the King of France! Now you know this is a lie; France no longer has a monarchy. And I know that you know I am lying but I don't care because I am not in your world of reality; I am in my fantasy world and in my world I rule as king.

It is important to note that the factors cited above can also contribute to a very satisfying and mentally sound adult life too.

The door swings both ways.

I now want to discuss a human trait that stems directly from our life of fantasy…BLAME!

Blame sucks and it sucks big time…

Blame Is A Useless Concept!

The cause of blame stems directly from our lives lived within our fantasies, where everything is perfect including you. But we all know in reality we are not perfect and as Nathaniel Hawthorne states in his book, "The Scarlet letter,' we are all broken pots.

But blame is a good example of manifested behavior spilling over from our fantasy existence. We cannot be at fault since we are perfect so others must be the cause. Blame is an excuse when all we really have are choices.

In my book "The Story of Stupid" http://www.amazon.com/dp/B007L2QCHK, I make this statement, "Life is tough; it's tougher if you are stupid." My statement isn't meant to be a putdown either. People have a tendency to making their lives tougher than what is warranted by living a lifestyle that is constantly in blame mode.

I have spent a good deal of my time in court for the sake of my patients. You only have to sit there and listen to the excuses defendants use in order to get released from charges or get bail. Some of these court sessions are better than comedy television. The defendant rarely admits to being at fault; but they have no compunction in blaming others for their deeds.

But like I said, we are all broken pots. We all have certain gifts and talents but many choose to envy the gifts and talents of others and blame their maladies on a variety of circumstances.

I can't sing and you know I can't dance and I don't look like Brad Pitt...sigh! I am just me and I have grown to accept me because no one does "ME" better than me!

I put myself through college as a standup comic and I can make people laugh and I have one of those personalities that think even gangrene is funny. My point is that you develop the talents you have been given and if you do this there is no reason to blame.

But in reality, there are a good many things we cannot become; and as people strive to become things they cannot or should not become, a certain envy develops and mostly from a lack of maturity described in Chapter 4. When this occurs, a person resorts to the blame game.

In consumerism, we have a similar situation occur which is called "scarcity thought". A person perceives that other people are getting what belongs to them and they want their issue. When they can't have what they perceive as theirs, they blame others for their lack.

The results of scarcity thought are massive consumer debt and financial meltdown into bankruptcy. Trying to keep up with the Joneses just doesn't work.

Next we have self-blame where we blame ourselves for things that occur in our lives that in reality, we didn't cause. Women are especially good at self-blame. A wife will blame herself when her mate strays into infidelity telling herself that she isn't pretty enough or sexy enough when in reality, the entire blame belongs solely to her husband. Infidelity is the result of a person embracing a lustful lifestyle and this is a person that really doesn't know what love is. And guess where lust is born? Yep, in a fantasy life!!!

There is another type of insidious blame that is the worst kind of blame. I call it "silent blame" and this is where a person harbors subconscious blame against another individual that doesn't necessarily manifest itself in outward behavior.

I had a patient that harbored ill feelings against her mother and blamed her for the breakup of a teenage relationship. A few years later she discovered her mother had nothing to do with her boyfriend breaking up with her but she still subconsciously blamed her mother because she couldn't accept the truth.

Outwardly she displayed a loving relationship with her mother but inwardly she harbored wrongful feelings. This resulted in low self-esteem and wrongful relationships that didn't last. She had been married three times and none of her marriages were long term. In other words, the manifested outward behavior was not against her mother but against her.

In working with her, I had to peel back the layers of her subconscious mind to find the root cause and she was amazed at what we both discovered in therapy sessions. Armed with the truth, she was able to finally put the resentment to rest.

I have taught you a lot of stuff and I know it can be overwhelming so you will need to re-read this book over and over again and commit it to memory but now let me sum it all up and define for you what I call the "Thoughts of a Fool" and is taken from my book of the same title: http://www.amazon.com/dp/B00CMK7CJS.

Chapter 4 – Thoughts of a Fool

Ah, the good life and what a life it would be if only we had the good life. But what is the good life? And how do we acquire it? And can this have anything to do with a con man's thinking that causes him/her to practice the con game?

Ancient Wisdom for Good Living

"What is the good life?" is a question as old as philosophy itself. In fact, it is the question that birthed philosophy as we know it. (1) Posed by ancient Greek thinkers and incorporated into the thought of Socrates through Plato, and then Aristotle, this question gets at the heart of human meaning and purpose. Why are we here, and since we are here, what are we to be doing? What is our meaning and purpose?

Out of the early Greek quest for the answer emerged two schools of thought. From Plato emerged rationalism: the good life consists of ascertaining unchanging ideals— justice, truth, goodness, beauty—those "forms" found in the ideal world. From Aristotle emerged empiricism: the good life consists of ascertaining knowledge through experience—what we can perceive of this world through our senses. (2)

For both Aristotle and Plato, rational thought used in contemplation of ideas is the substance of the good life. Despite the obvious emphasis by both on goodness emerging from the contemplative life of the mind (even though they disagreed on the source of rationality) both philosophers saw the good life as impacting and benefiting society. For Plato, society must emulate justice, truth, goodness, and beauty, so he constructs an ideal society. For Aristotle, virtue lived out in society is the substance of the good life, and well-being arises from well-doing.

Not long ago, I conducted an internet search on the tag "What is the good life?" and I was amazed at what came up as the top results of my search. Most of the entries involved shopping or consumption of one variety or another. Some entries were on locations to live, and still others involved self-help books or other media aimed at helping one construct a good life. Others were the names of stores selling goods to promote "the good life." There were no immediate entries on Plato, Aristotle, or the philosophical quest that they helped inaugurate. There were no results on wisdom or the quest for knowledge lived out in a virtuous life. Instead, most of the entries involved material pursuits and gains. Sadly, this reflects our modern definition of what is good.

Perhaps, what are for many individuals still very trying economic times; it is difficult not to equate material items with the good life, more money, more security, or more opportunity. While it has always been said of every generation that these are times of great crisis and upheaval, we feel this search for meaning anew and afresh today, and perhaps wonder at the practicality or wisdom of looking to the past for insight or understanding into the good life.

And yet, the ancients remind us that "not even when one has an abundance does one's life consist of possessions" (Luke 12:15). Abundant or meager as they may be, possessions must not make up the substance of one's life. Instead, their proper use necessarily involves right living in community. Perhaps the ancient Hebraic wisdom is particularly instructive in a time in which we might equate goodness with what we possess. "He has told you, *what is good*; and what does the Lord require of you but to do justice, to love kindness, and to walk humbly with your God?" (Micah 6:8) This vision of the good life, cast not when times were good, but during a time when calamity and exile awaited the nation of Israel offers an alternative understanding. Do justice, love kindness, and live out both of those virtues in light of humility before God; this is what is good and is the ground of the good life.

The wisdom of the ancients, from the Greeks and the Hebrews, suggests that the good life can be attained regardless of circumstance or possession. It shimmers in the wisdom of justice and kindness. It is found in the application of knowledge rightly applied in relationship

91

to the world around us. It shines in humility before the God who is *good*, and is part and parcel of a relationship with that God. The good life is not bought or sold; it is not a prime real estate location, or a formula for success. The good life is our life offered to God and to others in justice, kindness, and humility.

Margaret Manning is a member of the speaking and writing team at Ravi Zacharias International Ministries in Seattle, Washington.

(1) A.L. Herman, *The Ways of Philosophy: Searching for a Worthwhile Life* (Scholars Press: Atlanta, 1990), 1.
(2) *Ibid*, 82.

*****

The article above gets to the heart of the heart of the matter quickly.

We are going to be discussing various ideas of the good life and then center on what exactly the good life is.

I need my readers to focus on the misconceptions of the good life and why they have become the so-called definitions of the good life.

One of my most favorite adages is this: "The best lie is often sandwiched between two truths." The good life as you know it is a lie and I will prove this to you.

Is the Good Life Unchanging Ideals—Justice, Truth, Goodness, Beauty?

In Chapter 1, my goal was to lay a good foundation to behavioral science and teach you how the human mind functions and why you do the things you do. The mechanism of the human mind is the same for both genders but the way each gender employs there psyche is different.   There is no such thing as commercial versus personal mechanism of the mind. The human mind uses the same mechanism to make commercial decisions as well as personal decisions.

A good many of you would answer this question, "Is the Good Life Unchanging Ideals—Justice, Truth, Goodness, Beauty?" with a resounding "YES"! And you would be partially correct. The reason being is that your definition of justice, truth, goodness and beauty maybe skewed to the world's definition and not the correct definition.

Now take justice: recently as I write this the Boston Marathon bombers have been caught.   The older brother was killed and the younger brother was wounded and captured. In the course that followed, a series of tweets and Facebook posts have sided with the younger brother based on a series of conspiracy theories that these brothers were set up. They ignore the fact that the younger brother in custody has admitted and confessed to the bombings and has stated in his affidavit that no other entity influenced him or his brother. Even with his admission and confession, the conspiracy theories abound and justice is skewed as these people backing these conspiracy theories line up demanding the younger brother's release.

Let's take truth: in today's world truth is defined subjectively or in other words, truth is anything you want it to be. Objective or absolute truth never changes and it is this truth I am speaking about here. But truth can hurt and sometimes it hurts enough causing people to make their own truths to rationalize some really weird behavior.

How about goodness: this is without a doubt the most skewed definition of them all. Goodness to most people is defined as favorable action towards others and this is true but goodness is more of a complete lifestyle rather than simply action.

The following article discusses both good and evil and really gives a fine perspective on both subjects....

Good and Evil
From Wikipedia, the free encyclopedia
http://en.wikipedia.org/wiki/Good_and_evil

In many religions, angels are considered good beings. In the Judeo-Christian tradition, God —being the creator of all life —is seen as the personification of good.

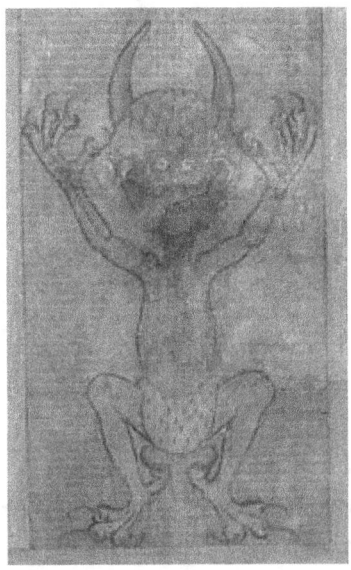

Satan, as seen in Codex Gigas. Demons are generally seen as evil beings, and Satan as greatest of these (in the Christian tradition).

In religion, ethics, and philosophy, the dichotomy **"good and evil"** refers to the location on a linear spectrum of objects, desires, or behaviors, the *good* direction being morally positive, and the *evil* direction morally negative.

In cultures with Manichaean and Abrahamic religious influence, evil is usually perceived as the dualistic antagonistic opposite of good, in which good should prevail and evil should be defeated. In cultures with

Buddhist spiritual influence, both good and evil are perceived as part of an antagonistic duality that itself must be overcome through achieving *Śūnyatā* meaning emptiness in the sense of recognition of good and evil being two opposing principles but not a reality, emptying the duality of them, and achieving a oneness.

Origin of the concept

Every language has a word expressing *good* in the sense of "having the right or desirable quality" (ἀρετή) and *bad* in the sense "undesirable". A sense of moral judgement and a distinction "right and wrong, good and bad" are cultural universals.

Ancient world

In the eastern part of ancient Persia almost five thousand years ago a religious philosopher called Zoroaster simplified the pantheon of early Iranian gods into two opposing forces: Ahura Mazda (Illuminating Wisdom) and Angra Mainyu (Destructive Spirit) which were in conflict.

For the western world, this idea developed into a religion which spawned many sects, some of which embraced an extreme dualistic belief that the material world should be shunned and the spiritual world should be embraced. Gnostic ideas influenced many ancient religions which teach that *gnosis* (variously interpreted as enlightenment, salvation, emancipation or 'oneness with God') may be reached by practicing philanthropy to the point of personal poverty, sexual abstinence (as far as possible for

96

hearers, total for *initiates*) and diligently searching for wisdom by helping others.

Classical world

In Western Civilization, the basic meanings of κακός and ἀγαθός are "bad, cowardly" and "good, brave, capable", and their absolute sense emerges only around 400 BC, with Pre-Socratic philosophy, in particular Democritus.

Morality in this absolute sense solidifies in the dialogues of Plato, together with the emergence of monotheistic thought (notably in *Euthyphro*, which ponders the concept of piety (τὸ ὅσιον) as a moral absolute). The idea is further developed in Late Antiquity by Neoplatonists, Gnostics, and Church Fathers.

This development from the relative or habitual to the absolute is also evident in the terms *ethics* and *morality* both being derived from terms for "regional custom", Greek ἦθος and Latin *mores*, respectively (see also *siðr*).

Medieval period

Medieval Christian philosophy was founded on the work of the Bishop Augustine of Hippo and theologian Thomas Aquinas who understood evil in terms of Biblical infallibility and Biblical inerrancy which they interpreted evil as the desire for anything remotely pleasurable to the human body.

Many medieval Christian theologians both broadened and narrowed the basic concept of *Good and evil* until it came to have several, sometimes complex definitions such as:

- a personal preference or subjective judgement regarding any issue which might be earn praise or punishment from the religious authorities
- religious obligation arising from Divine law leading to sainthood or damnation.
- a generally accepted cultural standard of behaviour which might enhance group survival or wealth
- natural law or behaviour which induces strong emotional reaction
- statute law imposing a legal duty

Modern Ideas

These basic ideas of a dichotomy have developed so that today:

- *Good* is a broad concept but it typically deals with an association with life, charity, continuity, happiness, love and justice.
- *Evil* is typically associated with conscious and deliberate wrongdoing, discrimination designed to harm others, humiliation of people designed to diminish their psychological needs and dignity, destructiveness, and acts of unnecessary and/or indiscriminate violence.
- the dilemma of the human condition and humans' and their capacity to perform both good and evil activities.

The nature of *being good* has been given many treatments; one is that the good is based on the natural love, bonding, and affection that begins at the earliest stages of personal development; another is that goodness is a product of knowing truth. Differing views also exist as to why evil might arise. Many religious and philosophical traditions claim that evil behavior is an *aberration* that results from the imperfect human condition (e.g. "The Fall of Man"). Sometimes, evil is attributed to the existence of free will and human agency. Some argue that evil itself is ultimately based in an ignorance of truth (i.e., human value, sanctity, divinity). A variety of Enlightenment thinkers have alleged the opposite, by suggesting that evil is learned as a consequence of tyrannical social structures.

Theories of moral goodness

Philosophers inquire into what sorts of things are good, and what the word "good" really means in the abstract. As a philosophical concept, goodness might represent a hope that natural love be *continuous, expansive,* and *all-inclusive.* In a monotheistic religious context, it is by this *hope* that an important concept of God is derived —as an infinite projection of love, manifest as goodness in the lives of people. In other contexts, the good is viewed to be whatever produces the best consequences upon the lives of people, especially with regard to their states of well being.

In religion, ethics, and philosophy, **goodness and evil**, or simply **good and evil**, refers to the concept of all human desires and behaviors as conforming to a *dualistic* *spectrum*—wherein in one direction are aspects that are *wisely reverent of life and continuity* ("good"), and in the other are aspects that are *vainly reverent of death and destruction* ("evil").

Religious and philosophical views tend to agree that, while "good and evil" is *a concept* and therefore *an abstraction*, **goodness** is intrinsic to human nature and is ultimately based on the natural love, bonding, affection that people grow to feel for other people. Likewise, most religious and philosophical interpretations agree that **evil** is ultimately based in an ignorance of truth (i.e. human value, sanctity, divinity), and evil behavior itself is an *aberration* —one that defies any understanding save that the path to evil is one of confusion and excessive desire (greed). In physics and statistical thermodynamics, the property of goodness or order is often referred to as a state of low entropy.

As a philosophical abstraction, goodness represents a hope that natural love be *continuous, expansive,* and *all-inclusive*. In religious context, it is by this *hope* that an important concept of God is derived —as an infinite projection of love, manifest as goodness in the lives of people. The belief in such hope is often translated as "faith", and wisdom itself is largely defined within religious doctrine as *a knowledge and understanding of innate goodness*. The concepts of innocence, spiritual purity, and salvation are likewise related to a concept of being in, or returning to, a state of *goodness*—one that, according to various teachings of "enlightenment", approaches a state of *holiness* (or Godliness*)*.

Descriptive, meta-ethical, and normative fields

It is possible to treat the essential theories of value by the use of a philosophical and academic approach. In properly analyzing theories of value, everyday beliefs are not only carefully *catalogued* and *described*, but also rigorously *analyzed* and *judged*.

There are at least two basic ways of presenting a theory of value, based on two different kinds of questions:

- What do people find good, and what do they despise?
- What really is good, and what really is bad?

The two questions are subtly different. One may answer the first question by researching the world by use of social science, and examining the preferences that people assert. However, one may answer the second question by use of reasoning, introspection, prescription, and generalization.

The former kind of method of analysis is called "descriptive", because it attempts to describe what people actually view as good or evil; while the latter is called "normative", because it tries to actively prohibit evils and cherish goods. These descriptive and normative approaches can be complementary. For example, tracking the decline of the popularity of slavery across cultures is the work of descriptive ethics, while advising that slavery be avoided is normative.

Meta-ethics is the study of the fundamental questions concerning the nature and origins of the good and the evil, including inquiry into the nature of good and evil, as well as the meaning of evaluative language. In this respect, meta-ethics is not necessarily tied to investigations into how others see the good, or of asserting what is good.

Theories of the intrinsically good

A satisfying formulation of goodness is valuable because it might allow one to construct a good life or society by reliable processes of deduction, elaboration, or prioritization. One could answer the ancient question, "How should we then live?" among many other important related questions. It has long been thought that this question can best be answered by examining what it is that necessarily makes a thing valuable, or in what the source of value consists.

Transcendental realism

One attempt to define goodness describes it as a property of the world. According to this claim, to talk about the good is to talk about something real that exists in the object itself, independent of the perception of it. Plato advocated this view, in his expression that there is such a thing as an eternal realm of forms or ideas, and that the greatest of the ideas and the essence of being was goodness, or The good.

The good was defined by many ancient Greeks and other ancient philosophers as a perfect and eternal idea, or blueprint. The good is the right relation between all that exists, and this exists in the mind of the Divine, or some heavenly realm. The good is the harmony of a just political community, love, friendship, the ordered human soul of virtues, and the right relation to the Divine and to Nature. The characters in Plato's dialogues mention the many virtues of a philosopher, or a lover of wisdom.

A theist is a person who believes that gods exist (monotheism or polytheism). A theist may, therefore, claim that the universe has a purpose and value according to the will of such creator(s) that lies partially beyond human understanding. For instance, Thomas Aquinas—a proponent of this view—believed he had proven the existence of God, and the right relations that humans ought to have to the divine first cause.

Monotheists might also hope for infinite universal love. Such hope is often translated as "faith", and wisdom itself is largely defined within some religious doctrines as *a knowledge and understanding of innate goodness.*

The concepts of innocence, spiritual purity, and salvation are likewise related to a concept of being in, or returning to, a state of *goodness*—one that, according to various teachings of "enlightenment", approaches a state of *holiness* (or Godliness*).* A dystheist or atheist, however, may potentially believe that the concept of goodness is not related to deities.

Perfectionism

Aristotle believed that virtues consisted of realization of potentials unique to humanity, such as the use of reason. This type of view, called perfectionism, has been recently defended in modern form by Thomas Hurka.

An entirely different form of perfectionism has arisen in response to rapid technological change. Some techno-optimists, especially transhumanists, avow a form of perfectionism in which the capacity to determine good and trade off fundamental values, is expressed not by humans but by software, genetic engineering of humans, artificial intelligence.

Skeptics assert that rather than perfect goodness, it would be only the appearance of perfect goodness, reinforced by persuasion technology and probably brute force of violent technological escalation, which would cause people to accept such rulers or rules authored by them.

Welfarist theories

Welfarist theories of value say things that are good are such because of their positive effects on human well-being.

Subjective theories of wellbeing

It is difficult to figure out where an immaterial trait such as "goodness" could reside in the world. A counterproposal is to locate values inside people. Some philosophers go so far as to say that if some state of affairs does not tend to arouse a desirable subjective state in self-aware beings, then it cannot be good.

Most philosophers that think goods have to create desirable mental states also say that goods are experiences of self-aware beings. These philosophers often distinguish the experience, which they call an intrinsic good, from the things that seem to cause the experience, which they call "inherent" goods. Failing to distinguish the two leads to a subject-object problem in which it is not clear who is evaluating what object.

Some theories describe no higher collective value than that of maximizing *pleasure* for individual(s). Some even define goodness and intrinsic value as the experience of pleasure, and bad as the experience of pain. This view is called hedonism, a *monistic theory of value*. It has two main varieties: simple, and Epicurean.

Simple hedonism is the view that physical pleasure is the ultimate good. However, the ancient philosopher Epicurus used the word 'pleasure' in a more general sense that encompassed a range of states from bliss to contentment to relief. Contrary to popular caricature, he valued pleasures of the mind to bodily pleasures, and advocated moderation as the surest path to happiness.

Jeremy Bentham's book *The Principles of Morals and Legislation* prioritized goods by considering pleasure, pain and consequences. This theory had a wide effect on public affairs, up to and including the present day. A similar system was later named Utilitarianism by John Stuart Mill. More broadly, utilitarian theories are examples of Consequentialism. All utilitarian theories are based upon the *maxim of utility*, which states that *good* is whatever provides *the greatest happiness for the greatest number*. It follows from this principle that what brings happiness to the greatest number of people is good.

A benefit of tracing good to pleasure and pain is that both are easily understandable, both in oneself and to an extent in others. For the hedonist, the explanation for helping behaviour may come in the form of *empathy*—the ability of a being to "feel" another's pain. People tend to value the lives of gorillas more than those of mosquitoes because the gorilla lives and feels, making it easier to empathize with them. This idea is carried forward in the ethical relationship view and has given rise to the animal rights movement and parts of the peace movement. The impact of sympathy on human behaviour is compatible with Enlightenment views, including David Hume's stances that the idea of a self with unique identity is illusory, and that morality ultimately comes down to sympathy and fellow feeling for others, or the exercise of approval underlying moral judgments.

A view adopted by James Griffin attempts to find a subjective alternative to hedonism as an intrinsic value. He argues that the satisfaction of one's informed desires constitutes well-being, whether or not these desires actually bring the agent happiness. Moreover, these preferences must be life-relevant, that is, contribute to the success of a person's life overall.

Desire satisfaction may occur without the agent's awareness of the satisfaction of the desire. For example, if a man wishes for his legal will to be enacted after his death, and it is, then his desire has been satisfied even though he will never experience or know of it.

106

Objective theories of wellbeing

The idea that the ultimate good exists and is not orderable but is globally measurable is reflected in various ways in economic (classical economics, green economics, welfare economics, Gross National Happiness) and scientific (positive psychology, the Science of morality) well-being measuring theories, all of which focus on various ways of assessing progress towards that goal, a so-called Genuine Progress Indicator. Modern economics thus reflects very ancient philosophy, but a calculation or quantitative or other process based on cardinality and statistics replaces the simple ordering of values.

For example, in both economics and in folk wisdom, the value of something seems to rise so long as it is relatively scarce. However, if it becomes too scarce, it leads often to a conflict, and can reduce collective value.

In the classical political economy of Adam Smith and David Ricardo, and in its critique by Karl Marx, *human labor* is seen as the ultimate source of all new economic value. This is an *objective* theory of value (see value theory), which attributes value to real production-costs, and ultimately expenditures of human labor-time (see also law of value).

It contrasts with marginal utility theory, which argues that the value of labor depends on subjective preferences by consumers, which may however also be objectively studied.

The economic value of labor may be assessed technically in terms of its use-value or utility or commercially in terms of its exchange-value, price or production cost (see also labor power. But its value may also be socially assessed in terms of its contribution to the wealth and well-being of a society.

In non-market societies, labor may be valued primarily in terms of skill, time, and output, as well as moral or social criteria and legal obligations. In market societies, labor is valued economically primarily through the labor market.

The price of labor may then be set by supply and demand, by strike action or legislation, or by legal or professional entry-requirements into occupations.

Mid-range theories

Conceptual metaphor theories argue against both subjective and objective conceptions of value and meaning, and focus on the relationships between body and other essential elements of human life. In effect, conceptual metaphor theories treat ethics as an ontology problem and the issue of how to work-out values as a negotiation of these metaphors, not the application of some abstraction or a strict standoff between parties who have no way to understand each other's views.

Goodness and agency
Agent-centered theories

One more recent philosophical proposal has defined good as "That which increases the quality and quantity of choices available overall." These approaches have been called *choice optimization theories*. This maxim might be countered by the phenomenon of opportunity costs observed by social scientists. Opportunity cost is when people who are confronted with a greater number of choices also experience greater dismay at their choices after the fact, because of the missed opportunities.

In his *Development as Freedom*, Amartya Sen asserted free time as the most fundamental good, and systems of organizing that enabled it as the most fundamental value in civilization. He refuted the common claim that Asian value theorists had devalued freedom and was clear that a marketplace (creating unity via pricing) valuing free time could be created. Marilyn Waring took a similar view from a feminist perspective, arguing women's time was undervalued and especially the free time they used to raise and teach children. Waring also strongly denied that military hardware or activities were of any value, and attempted to reconcile peace or welfare views of good with the ecological values.

Other agent-centered theories amongst contemporary thinkers such as Bernard Williams seek to revive the old concept (associated for example with Aristotle and Confucius, that the right action is the action that a person of good character (the "great-souled man" as Aristotle said) will perform.

Goodwill

John Rawls' book *A Theory of Justice* prioritized social arrangements and goods based on their contribution to justice. Rawls defined justice as *fairness*, especially in distributing social goods, defined fairness in terms of procedures, and attempted to prove that just institutions and lives are good, if rational individuals' goods are considered fairly. Rawls's crucial invention was the original position, a procedure in which one tries to make objective moral decisions by refusing to let personal facts about oneself enter one's moral calculations.

One problem with the thinkings of Rawls is that it is overly procedural. Procedurally fair processes of the type used by Rawls may not leave enough room for judgment, and therefore, reduce the totality of goodness. For example, if two people are found to own an orange, the standard fair procedure is to cut it in two and give half to each. However, if one wants to eat it while the other wants the rind to flavor a cake, cutting it in two is clearly less good than giving the peel to the baker and feeding the core to the eater.

Applying procedural fairness to an entire society therefore seems certain to create recognizable inefficiencies and therefore be unfair, and (by the equivalence of justice with fairness) unjust.

However, procedural processes are not always necessarily damning in this way. Immanuel Kant, a great influence for Rawls, similarly applies a lot of procedural practice within the practical application of *The Categorical Imperative*; however, this is indeed not based solely on 'fairness'. Even though an example like the one above regarding the orange would not be something that required the practical application of *The Categorical*

Imperative, it is important to draw distinction between Kant and Rawls, and note that Kant's Theory would not necessarily lead to the same problems Rawls' does — i.e., the cutting in half of the orange. Kant's Theory promotes acting out of Duty — acting for the Summum Bonum for him, *The Good Will* - and in fact encourages Judgement, too. What this would mean is that the outcome of the Orange's distribution would not be such a simple process for Kant as the reason why it would be wanted by both parties would necessarily have to be a part of the Judgement process, thus eliminating the problem that Rawls' account suffers here.

Agent-external theories
Society, life and ecology

Many views value *unity* as a good: to go beyond eudaimonia by saying that an individual person's flourishing is valuable only as a means to the flourishing of society as a whole. In other words, a single person's life is, ultimately, not important or worthwhile in itself, but is good only as a means to the success of society as a whole. Some elements of Confucianism are an example of this, encouraging the view that people ought to conform as individuals to demands of a peaceful and ordered society.

According to the naturalistic view, the flourishing of society is not, or not the only, intrinsically good thing. Defenses of this notion are often formulated by reference to biology, and observations that living things compete more with their own kind than with other kinds. Rather, what is of intrinsic good is the flourishing of all sentient

111

life, extending to those animals that have some level of similar sentience, such as Great Ape personhood. Others go farther, declaring that life itself is of intrinsic value.

By another approach, one achieves peace and agreement by focusing, not on one's peers (who may be rivals or competitors), but on the common environment. The reasoning: As living beings it is clearly and objectively good that we are surrounded by an ecosystem that supports life. Indeed, if we weren't, we could neither discuss that good nor even recognize it. The anthropic principle in cosmology recognizes this view.

Under materialism or even embodiment values, or in any system that recognizes the validity of ecology as a scientific study of limits and potentials, an ecosystem is a fundamental good. To all who investigate, it seems that goodness, or value, exists within an ecosystem, Earth. Creatures within that ecosystem and wholly dependent on it, evaluate good relative to what else could be achieved there. In other words, good is situated in a particular place and one does not dismiss everything that is not available there (such as very low gravity or absolutely abundant sugar candy) as "not good enough", one works within its constraints. Transcending them and learning to be satisfied with them, is thus another sort of value, perhaps called satisfaction, or in Buddhism, enlightenment.

Values and the people that hold them seem necessarily subordinate to the ecosystem. If this is so, then what kind of being could validly apply the word "good" to an ecosystem as a whole? Who would have the power to assess and judge an ecosystem as good or bad? By what criteria? And by what criteria would ecosystems be modified, especially larger ones such as the atmosphere (climate change) or oceans (extinction) or forests (deforestation)?

"Remaining on Earth" as the most basic value. While green ethicists have been most forthright about it, and have developed theories of Gaia philosophy, biophilia, bioregionalism that reflect it, the questions are now universally recognized as central in determining value, e.g. the economic "value of Earth" to humans as a whole, or the "value of life" that is neither whole-Earth nor human. Many have come to the conclusion that without assuming ecosystem continuation as a universal good, with attendant virtues like biodiversity and ecological wisdom it is impossible to justify such operational requirements as sustainability of human activity on Earth.

One response is that humans are not necessarily confined to Earth, and could use it and move on. A counter-argument is that only a tiny fraction of humans could do this—and they would be self-selected by ability to do technological escalation on others (for instance, the ability to create large spacecraft to flee the planet in, and simultaneously fend off others who seek to prevent them). Another counter-argument is that extraterrestrial life would encounter the fleeing humans and destroy them as a locust species. A third is that if there are no other worlds fit to support life (and no extraterrestrials who compete with humans to occupy them) it is both futile to flee, and foolish to imagine that it would take less energy and skill to protect the Earth as a habitat than it would take to construct some new habitat.

Accordingly remaining on Earth, as a living being surrounded by a working ecosystem, is a fair statement of the most basic values and goodness to any being we are able to communicate with. A moral system without this axiom seems simply not actionable.

However, most religious systems acknowledge an afterlife and improving this is seen as an even more basic good. In many other moral systems, also, remaining on Earth in a state that lacks honor or power over self is less desirable — consider seppuku in bushido, kamikazes or the role of suicide attacks in Jihadi rhetoric. In all these systems, remaining on Earth is perhaps no higher than a third-place value.

Radical values environmentalism can be seen as either a very old or a very new view: that the only intrinsically good thing is a flourishing ecosystem; individuals and societies are merely instrumentally valuable, good only as means to having a flourishing ecosystem. The Gaia philosophy is the most detailed expression of this overall thought but it strongly influenced Deep Ecology and the modern Green Parties.

It is often claimed that aboriginal peoples never lost this sort of view. Anthropological linguistics studies links between their languages and the ecosystems they lived in, which gave rise to their knowledge distinctions. Very often, environmental cognition and moral cognition were not distinguished in these languages. Offenses to nature

114

were like those to other people, and Animism reinforced this by giving nature "personality" via myth. Anthropological theories of value explore these questions.

Most people in the world reject older situated ethics and localized religious views. However small-community-based and ecology-centric views have gained some popularity in recent years. In part, this has been attributed to the desire for ethical certainties. Such a deeply rooted definition of goodness would be valuable because it might allow one to construct a good life or society by reliable processes of deduction, elaboration or prioritization. Ones that relied only on local referents one could verify for oneself, creating more certainty and therefore less investment in protection, hedging and insuring against consequences of loss of the value.

History and novelty

An event is often seen as being of value simply because of its *novelty* in fashion and art. By contrast, cultural history and other antiques are sometimes seen as of value in and of themselves due to their *age*. Philosopher-historians Will and Ariel Durant spoke as much with the quote, "As the sanity of the individual lies in the continuity of his memories, so the sanity of the group lies in the continuity of its traditions; in either case a break in the chain invites a neurotic reaction" (The Lessons of History, 72).

Assessment of the value of old or historical artifacts takes into consideration, especially but not exclusively: the value placed on having a detailed knowledge of the past, the desire to have tangible ties to ancestral history, and/or the increased market value scarce items traditionally hold.

Creativity and innovation and invention are sometimes upheld as fundamentally good especially in Western industrial society — all imply newness, and even opportunity to profit from novelty. Bertrand Russell was notably pessimistic about creativity and thought that knowledge expanding faster than wisdom necessarily was fatal.

Goodness and morality in biology

The issue of good and evil in the human makeup, often associated with morality, is regarded by some biologists (notably Edward O. Wilson, Jeremy Griffith, David Sloan Wilson and Frans de Waal) as an important question to be addressed by the field of biology.

*****

The ancient Geeks viewed goodness and beauty as paramount to the foundational base of their society. There is a saying, "The grandeur that was Greece and the glory that was Rome," and this is basically true.

The ancient Greeks had a tremendously "skewed' view of the world. On their battle shields they emblazoned symbols of peace on weapons of war. Their ideals did not match their actions and their quest or empire proved this fact.

Any moral act, whether good or bad is defined by action and not just by words. There is a bible story that describes this fact:

"But what do you think? A man had two sons. He went to the first and said, 'Son, go and work in the vineyard today.' His son replied, 'I don't want to,' but later he changed his mind and went. Then the father went to the other son and told him the same thing. He replied, 'I will, sir,' but he didn't go. Which of the two did the father's will?" They answered, "The first." Jesus said to them, "Truly I tell you, tax collectors and prostitutes will get into God's kingdom ahead of you. Matthew 21: 28-31

Action speaks louder than words!!!

Chapter 5 – How to Spot a Con Man

Secrets, lies and tricks are tactics many con artists use to manipulate people to get what they want, oftentimes destroying their victim's lives forever. Con artists gain a person's confidence so they can have easy access to the victim's money, trust and friendship. To avoid being fooled by a con artists look out for the following warning signs:

Blending In
Effective con artists must disguise their true motives. They try hard to look and talk like others in the community and quickly get to know a lot of people.

Talking the Talk
Con artists learn vocabulary so they sound knowledgeable in the subject they are talking about.

Dressing for Success

Con artists want others to believe that they are regular folks, but they work hard to come across as smooth, professional and successful.

Bringing out the Worst in You

Con artists often expose your negative traits such as greed, fear and insecurity. They know that big promises with no risk get people's attention. They also try and make you feel inadequate if you don't believe what they are telling you, or are asking too many questions.

Fair-Weather Friends

At the beginning, con artists are very friendly and take a personal interest in you. After they get what they want, con artists minimize their contact with you.

Moving Frequently

Even the best con artists can only play the part for so long before people become suspicious of their behaviors and motives.

To ensure that you never fall victim to the scam of a con artist, don't trust a person too easily. Always do your homework and investigate a person and the claims he/she is making before giving him/her your money or signing a contract. If you fear you may be dealing with a con, stop speaking with the person and do not give him/her any personal information.

Red Flags

If you've already entered into a transaction with someone, keep an eye out for the following warning signs:

- Secrecy - Are you asked not to tell anyone?
- Cash only - Many (but not all) con artists don't like to be paid by check because it leaves a paper trail.
- Jackpot just around the corner - The con artist is stringing you along while he or she collects more money from you (e.g. "Any day now..."). Your own denial might allow this procrastination to go on far longer than common sense would allow, because you don't want to face the possibility that you've been duped.
- Procrastination turns into intimidation - When your patience runs thin and you begin to question the con artist's credibility, you may end up getting treated like a traitor, or even a fool. They might try to intimidate you so you'll stick around until they can flee with the money. (E.g. "You're as guilty as I am in this.")

Know Your Own Weaknesses

These are the characteristics and situations that con artists most often exploit:

- Loneliness
- Sense of charity
- Desperation regarding money (e.g. heavily indebted, business financial problems)
- Being unhappy with your life, and a tendency to look for a "quick fix"
- Falling in love (If a new romantic interest wants you to throw in your lot with theirs, get a second

opinion! Ask your family and professionals for their advice.)

Common Scams

- Home improvement - repairs or improvements you don't need
- Bank - false bank examiner; the con artist asks the victim (usually an older widow) to test the honesty of employees by withdrawing substantial funds, which are given to the con artist for "examination". The victim is given a fake receipt and the con artist disappears with the cash.
- Investment - franchises, vending machines, land frauds, theft of inventions, securities investments, work-at-home
- Postal frauds - chain letters, magazine subscriptions, unordered merchandise, correspondence courses
- Others: bait and switch, charity rackets, computer dating, debt consolidation, contracts, dance lessons, freezer plans, psychic fraud, fortune tellers, health clubs, job placement, lonely hearts, medical quackery, missing heirs, referral sales, talent scouts, pyramid schemes, fake officials.

Sociopaths use flattery and inflated credentials. They talk fast, pushing you for fast decisions

Sooner or later, you will have a run-in with a sociopath. There are just too many of them—possibly between 3 million and 12 million sociopaths in America. And they aren't necessarily locked up in jail. Sociopaths roam

121

through all parts of society, all areas of the country, all walks of life.

There is only one way to protect yourself from sociopaths: You must know what they are, and put your guard up when you start seeing the symptoms.

Sociopaths are prolific con artists. Here are some typical con artist tricks.

Lavish flattery

If you've just met someone who is overwhelming you with praise, attention and concern, be careful. Be particularly careful if you're lonely and looking for love—con artists know exactly how to play that tune.

Credentials—exaggerated and fabricated

Con artists may "prove" themselves by namedropping or volunteering detailed resumes or credentials. If you're at all suspicious, check their references.

Building your trust

Con artists will sometimes honor their commitments in the beginning so that you begin to trust them. They'll pay back initial loans, or appear to be unselfishly helping other people. Their objective is to get you to drop your guard.

The story doesn't quite add up

The con artist's story may have small inconsistencies or unexplained loose ends. If you ask questions, the con will glibly provide an explanation—which may also not add up. Or, he or she will sidestep the issue by accusing you of paranoia or mistrust.

"I need an answer now."

A crisis needs to be averted, an opportunity will disappear—whatever the reason, a con artist will want an answer right away. If you have time to think, research or ask advice, you may realize that con artist's plan is a ploy. The con will want your money before you figure it out.

Intense eye contact

Typically, when people talk to each other, they look each other in the eyes and then briefly look away. Sociopathic con artists often exhibit a "predatory stare"—unblinking, fixated and emotionless. It's not a sign of empathy—it's an effort to assert control.

Isolation

Con artists will slowly and subtly separate you from people who may question their plans. They may intercept phone calls from your friends. They may refuse to associate with your family. They'll tell you, "It's you and me against the world, baby." Soon, you're alone with them, snared in their net.

*****

My goal was to give you salient information to consider that will prevent you from being the victim of any Type 1 or Type 2 Con artist.

I sincerely hope my words hold value and worth to you. If you have any questions please write to me at mailto:lee.benton@epybealth.com.

I answer all of my emails and actually quite enjoy engaging my readers.

Now I have a special gift for you...read on.

I Have a Special Gift for My Readers

I appreciate my readers for without them I am just another author attempting to make a difference. If my book has made a favorable impression please leave me an honest review. Thank you in advance for you participation.

My readers and I have in common a passion for the written word as well as the desire to learn and grow from books.

My special offer to you is a massive ebook library that I have compiled over the years. It contains hundreds of fiction and non-fiction ebooks in Adobe Acrobat PDF format as well as the Greek classics and old literary classics too.

In fact, this library is so massive to completely download the entire library will require over 5 GBs open on your desktop.

Use the link below and scan all of the ebooks in the library. You can select the ebooks you want individually or download the entire library.

The link below does not expire after a given time period so you are free to return for more books rather than clog your desktop. And feel free to give the link to your friends who enjoy reading too.

I thank you for reading my book and hope if you are pleased that you will leave me an honest review so that I can improve my work and or write books that appeal to your interests.

Okay, here is the link…

http://tinyurl.com/special-readers-promo

PS: If you wish to reach me personally for any reason you may simply write to mailto:support@epubwealth.com.

I answer all of my emails so rest assured I will respond.

Meet the Author

Dr. Leland Benton is Director of Applied Web Info, a holding company for ePubWealth.com, a leading ePublisher company based in Utah. With over 21,000 resellers in over 22-countries, ePubWealth.com is a leader in ePublishing, book promotion, and ebook marketing.

As the creator and author of "The ePubWealth Program," Leland teaches up-and-coming authors the ins-and-outs of today's ePublishing world. He has assisted hundreds of authors make it big in the ePublishing world.

Leland also created a series of external book promotion programs and teaches authors how to promote their books using external marketing sources.

Leland is also the Managing Director of Applied Mind Sciences, the company's mind research unit and Chief Forensics Investigator for the company's ForensicsNation unit. He is active in privacy rights through the company's PrivacyNations unit and is an expert in survival planning and disaster relief through the company's SurvivalNations unit.

Leland resides in Southern Utah.

Visit some of his websites
http://appliedmindsciences.com/
http://appliedwebinfo.com/
http://BoolbuilderPLUS.com

http://embarrassingproblemsfix.com/
http://www.epubwealth.com/
http://forensicsnation.com/
http://neternatives.com/
http://privacynations.com/
http://survivalnations.com/
http://thebentonkitchen.com
http://theolegions.org

www.ingramcontent.com/pod-product-compliance
Lightning Source LLC
Chambersburg PA
CBHW070924290526
45795CB00001B/418